Describing Cinema

T0384200

Describing Cinema

TIMOTHY CORRIGAN

OXFORD
UNIVERSITY PRESS

OXFORD
UNIVERSITY PRESS

Oxford University Press is a department of the University of Oxford. It furthers
the University's objective of excellence in research, scholarship, and education
by publishing worldwide. Oxford is a registered trade mark of Oxford University
Press in the UK and certain other countries.

Published in the United States of America by Oxford University Press
198 Madison Avenue, New York, NY 10016, United States of America.

© Oxford University Press 2024

Library of Congress Cataloging-in-Publication Data
Names: Corrigan, Timothy, 1951– author.
Title: Describing cinema / Timothy Corrigan.
Description: New York, NY : Oxford University Press, [2024] |
Includes bibliographical references.
Identifiers: LCCN 2023038556 (print) | LCCN 2023038557 (ebook) |
ISBN 9780197625354 (hardback) | ISBN 9780197625361 (paperback) |
ISBN 9780197625385 (epub)
Subjects: LCSH: Film criticism. | Motion pictures—Philosophy. |
Motion pictures—Aesthetics. | Motion pictures—Appreciation.
Classification: LCC PN1995 .C654 2024 (print) | LCC PN1995 (ebook) |
DDC 791.4301—dc23/eng/20231011
LC record available at https://lccn.loc.gov/2023038556
LC ebook record available at https://lccn.loc.gov/2023038557

DOI: 10.1093/oso/9780197625354.001.0001

Paperback printed by Marquis Book Printing, Canada
Hardback printed by Bridgeport National Bindery, Inc., United States of America

Contents

Preface

Describing Cinema is part analysis, part rhetoric, and part pedagogy. It examines and demonstrates acts of describing scenes, shots,
and sequences in films, as probably the most common and the most
underestimated way viewers respond to movies. Practiced energet-
ically and carefully, descriptions become exceptionally rich ways to
demonstrate and celebrate the activities, varieties, and challenges
of a central generative movement in the viewing and interpretation
of films. Acts of describing films or parts of films can measure and
instantiate complex ways of seeing that are partly about accuracy
but equally about the mobility of understanding and interpretation.
At its best, describing films never simply denotes actions, images,
sounds, or styles but rather orchestrates any combination of
those dimensions—along with other dimensions, such as readings,
memories, and off-screen experiences—as an intersubjective and
sometimes creative movement between films, viewers, and a rhetorical language. Here, especially, writing about film (or talking
about film) becomes thinking about films and, at the same time,
thinking about myself experiencing those films.

In a sense, this may be a book more about language than about
the films themselves, or at least about a more lively, more dynamic
meeting of the two as they encounter each other through a viewer.
This is a book about an interpretive language and an effort to open
that language, to loosen it, to flex words as they encounter specific
parts or wholes of a film. This is a book about that language as a
visible extension of my own subjectivity, as certain films elicit a
network or "spiderweb" of meanings. My choices of films and specific sequences are, from one angle, a product of that subjectivity,

as is the recurrence of certain figures and motifs across these sixteen short essays. These are some films and some sequences that have especially moved me through film history since that watershed decade of the 1940s. This is a different kind of writing about film.

Acknowledgments

Throughout the writing of this book, I have benefitted from conversations with my gracious colleagues in the Penn Cinema and Media Studies department, with Kyle Stevens who helped lift the early idea off the ground, and with Alan Singer who, so typically, illuminated the larger implications of what this book wants to be about. The students and faculty at Charles University in Prague, and at the University of Chicago provided dynamic forums where I presented early versions of the material. At Oxford University Press, Norm Hirschy encouraged the project from the beginning and two anonymous readers helped to polish it through its final stages. Closer to home, I have been fortunate to be surrounded by a family of smart, creative, and generous readers and interlocutors: Anna Corrigan, Graham Corrigan, Cecilia Corrigan, Marcia Ferguson, and M. Carr Ferguson. Thank you, one and all.

PART I

IN OTHER WORDS: FILM AND THE SPIDER WEB OF DESCRIPTION

Properly written texts are like spiders' webs: tight, concentric, transparent, well-spun and firm. They draw into themselves all the creatures of the air. Metaphors flitting hastily through them become their nourishing prey. Subject matter comes winging towards them. The soundness of a conception can be judged by whether it causes one quotation to summon another. Where thought has opened up one cell of reality, it should, without violence by the subject,

Describing Cinema. Timothy Corrigan, Oxford University Press. © Oxford University Press 2024.
DOI: 10.1093/oso/9780197625354.003.0001

penetrate the next. It proves its relation to the object as soon as other objects crystallize around it. In the light that it casts on its chosen substance, others begin to glow.

—T. W. Adorno, *Minima Moralia:*
Reflections from Damaged Life, 87

Pour qu'une chose soit intéressante, il suffit de la regarder longtemps.

—Gustave Flaubert, Correspondence, 1845, I, 192

Far behind the eye the quest begins.

—Samuel Beckett, "Mal vu mal dit,"
The Grove Centenary Edition, Vol. 4, 468

Early in Cornell Woolrich's 1942 short story, originally titled "It Had to Be Murder," the narrator Jeffries, with "his movements . . . strictly limited," watches, out the bay window of his bedroom, the daily routines of his neighbors in the windows across a courtyard separating him from them.[1] One particular neighbor attracts his attention:

> I couldn't make out what he was doing at first. He seemed to be busy in a perpendicular, up-and-down way rather than lengthwise. He remained in one place, but he kept dipping down out of sight and then straightening up into view again, at irregular intervals. It was almost like some sort of callisthenic exercise, except that the dips and rises weren't evenly timed enough for that. Sometimes he'd stay down a long time, sometimes he'd bob right up again, sometimes he'd go down two or three times in rapid succession. There was some sort of a widespread black V railing

---

[1] Note that the spelling of Jeffries's name in the short story differs from the spelling in the film as Jefferies.

him off from the window. Whatever it was, there was just a sliver of it showing above the upward inclination to which the window still deflected my line of vision. All it did was strike off the bottom of his undershirt, to the extent of a sixteenth of an inch maybe. But I haven't seen it there at other times, and I couldn't tell what it was.

Suddenly he left it for the first time since the shades had gone up, came out around it to the outside, stooped down into another part of the room, and straightened again with an armful of what looked like varicolored pennants at the distance at which I was. He went back behind the V and allowed them to fall across the top of it for a moment, and stay that way. He made one of his dips down out of sight and stayed that way a good while. (6)

The passage is particularly rich with verbal precision and metaphoric nuance, made all-the-more lively (and potentially all-the-more meaningful) by the fact that Jeffries is not at all certain what he is seeing in the cryptic and abstract movements across the distance. The source text for Alfred Hitchcock's 1954 meta-cinematic *Rear Window*, Woolrich's story continues to describe the mysterious visual movements of his neighbor with comparable linguistic dynamics, as the active field of what Jeffries calls the "delayed action" of moving between seeing, describing, and interpreting. Gradually, this "delayed action" uncovers Thorwald's murder of his wife, but, more importantly for my purposes, it also dramatizes the intricate relationship binding a concentrated viewing of images with their linguistic descriptions. In the pursuit of moving images, here the "delayed action" of description recognizes itself in a belated position of always being "too late," a position full of, on the one hand, interpretive potential and, on the other, even more complex challenges which, when the frame of the rear window becomes the "too late" moving images of *Vertigo*, threaten to transform that potential into swirling silences.

The Pedagogy of Description

For many years, I have been intrigued by the ways we respond and react to the movies: how we are mesmerized by them, how we are repulsed by them, how they make us think, how they allow us not to think, how they confuse us, how they challenge us to see different worlds and people, and how they ask us to see the world in different ways. Indeed, how many times do we finish watching a film and begin, as part of our response, what is often the difficult task of recounting a scene that fascinated us or a sequence that confused us?

Leaving aside for now the contemporary advantage of reviewing or rewatching parts of film through a DVD, a streaming site, or other technological replays, imagine this: immediately after watching a film, describe a favorite moment, a key scene, some important dialogue, or a particularly memorable sequence in that film. Better yet, make it a more measured and rhetorical challenge that involves a circle of viewers asked to write down individual descriptions of a specific part of a film. Doubtless, for different individuals, certain details will recur or overlap in their various descriptions, and other details will, more or less, differ. And, of course, some details may simply vanish from memory. The language of those descriptions could also vary considerably, and in some cases acts of concrete, denotative description may shift into slightly interpretive, connotative commentaries. To be sure, these descriptions will invariably be informed by the viewer's experiences and knowledge, which might include personal histories, critical readings, and recollections of other films; and some of these descriptions may even stray into more conceptual reflections on what individuals see and what it may mean in a larger aesthetic framework. No doubt questions of interpretation and meaning hover here but, only I'd argue, primarily as fluctuating and mobile consequences of those descriptions.

What this exercise—or "play" in a Derridean sense—underlines, I believe, is the extent to which "describing cinema" is a fundamental way that viewers respond to movies. We are all film describers in one way or another: when we leave a movie theater or end a video streaming, even though we have seen the same film as our companions, there is usually an inclination to talk about it in ways that extend well beyond thumbs up or thumbs down. This inclination can often extend to emailing our views to friends or even a more formalized blogging about what we've seen and how we evaluate a certain film. For me, these efforts to describe or "cite" the images or sequences that we have seen and have affected us when watching a film demonstrate the central activities, varieties, and challenges of watching movies. Whether it's a casual or concentrated response, describing a film or key parts of one becomes a central movement in spectatorship where language can not only reflect but also generate often different interpretations of that film.

In my role as a professor, description has been an important exercise, serving as one of the core assignments and strategies in virtually every film course I have taught. Aiming to have students move beyond simply "what happens" in a movie, I begin by asking them temporarily to set the story of the film aside or at least make it a secondary, delayed layer. Primarily my goal for this exercise is to promote attention and accuracy in how students look at the texture of images and sounds, a goal that most students quickly realize encounters significant resistance because of the excesses of the moving image with its numerous layers and multiple pieces. Discussing his experience with teaching film analysis, *Cahier du cinéma* critic Serge Daney characterizes that goal as a countercurrent to the popular certainties of cinephilia, a way that distances a viewer from the mesmerizing powers of a film and from its dominant hermeneutical models:

> To hold onto an audience of students in order to delay the moment when they would risk passing too quickly from one image to another, from one sound to another, seeing too quickly, declaring themselves prematurely, thinking they are done with

images and sounds when they don't suspect to what extent the arrangement of those images and sounds is something very complex and serious, and not at all innocent. School permits us to turn cinephilia against itself, to turn it inside out, like a glove, and to take our time about it. It confronts enigmas by not losing sight of them, holding onto them with one's eyes, keeping them. (91-92)

Inside and outside the classroom, this "not losing sight of" and "holding onto" the visual and aural enigmas of the cinema is, for me, the salient power of description as an always contingent, provisional, and sometimes creative response to the movies. Or, as Mark Doty puts it, in a much broader discussion in his book *The Art of Description*: all descriptions "are partial; thus all perception might be said to be tentative, an opportunity for interpretation, a guessing game." Suspended before and between attention and resistance, he continues: "What we want when we describe is surely complex: To solve the problem of speechlessness, which is a state without agency, so that we feel impressed upon by things but unable to push back at them" (5, 9).[2] Describing cinema might indeed be a kind of guessing game within the silence of spectatorship, and, in the short essays that follow this chapter, I occasionally signal that linguistic tentativeness with words and phrases such as "perhaps," "maybe," and "it seems," as well as by extended dependent clauses, repetitions, and open-ended questions, working to catch up with the moving image and its sounds.

[2] It should be clear, I hope, that this perspective here has little to do with Clifford Geertz's championing of so-called thick description over thin description, except perhaps to merge that distinction. With films, surface description has the same capacity to open up knowledge as thick description.

Ekphrasis and Description

The historical backdrop for the complexities of describing cinema begins with the notion of "ekphrasis," the term used to characterize the representational movement of a shared subject between different media, most often between a visual representation and a verbal representation. One of the earliest, and still best known, examples associated with ekphrasis is the poetic description of the image of "The Shield of Achilles" in Homer's *Iliad*, but the history and tradition of ekphrasis regularly appears as a dramatic and creative rhetorical action in literature from John Keat's "Grecian Urn," to the novels of Henry James, to Wallace Stevens's poetic efforts to "make the visible a little hard to see" ("The Creation of Sounds" 275) through to more recent encounters, such as the novels of W. G. Sebald, where resonant photographs punctuate and sometimes counterpoint the narrative prose. More to the point of my argument, cinematic versions of ekphrasis have also proliferated through the twentieth century, notably in literature that assimilates or adapts filmic grammars and perspectives: Luigi Pirandello's *Shoot!* (1915), Vladimir Nabokov's *Laughter in the Dark* (1932), or the contemporary poetry of John Ashberry are only a few notable examples of the range of works that, through an array of different strategies and goals, attempt to translate the cinematic into the literary. As varied as these practices and critical perspectives are, they sketch the historical and representational foundation that underpins the interaction of images and words, a foundation that remains a primary part of the heritage of describing cinema and its strategies to create, to release, or to spin verbal webs around, into, or after moving images. In all these cases and certainly in ways that haunt the description of film images, as W. J. T Mitchell notes, "The ekphrastic image acts . . . like a sort of unapproachable and unpresentable 'black hole' in the verbal structure, entirely absent from it, but shaping and affecting it in fundamental ways" (158).

Recent studies have both assimilated and expanded the dynamics of the ekphrastic, specifically in terms of the broader field of description and the multiple dimensions and places where description appears. In a 2016 issue of *Representation* titled "Description Across Disciplines," for instance, Sharon Marcus, Heather Love, and Stephen Best broaden significantly the field of ekphrasis (while, curiously, never referring to its long history) in their introduction, "Building a Better Description," where they highlight several of the key points made by the different essays in the volume, including the following:

- The generative flexibility of description and its "essential generosity" to attend "not only to its object but also to the collective, uncertain, and ongoing activity of trying to get a handle on the world."
- The interactivity of interpretation and description as "mutually interdependent."
- The productive relationship of description and subjectivity according to which description is a report not only of "what we encounter but also of ourselves encountering." (4, 8)

Each of these points—an uncertain generosity, a mutual interdependence, and a reflexive subjectivity embedded in the act of description—signal key elaborations in the transition from ekphrasis as act of transposition to description as an act of uncertain re-inscription whereby description becomes a dialogic re-inscription of self. Here the question of an accurate denotation of a source text in its ekphrastic recuperation gives way to its inevitable re-inscription within a continual chain of descriptive and subjective connotations. As Roland Barthes famously puts it in a manner that undercuts the lure of denotation in ekphrasis, "Structurally, the existence of two supposedly different systems—denotation and connotation—enables the text to operate like a game, each system referring to the other according to the requirements of a certain illusion. . . . [D]enotation is not the final meaning, but pretends to be so; under this illusion, it is ultimately no more than the last of the connotations (the one that seems both to establish and close the reading)" (*S/Z* 9).

Midway through Hitchcock's Vertigo, *Scottie's friend and former romantic partner, Midge, paints her face into her version of the portrait of Carlotta, the ghostly woman who haunts Scottie. It is an odd version of ekphrasis in which Midge describes and re-inscribes herself within the eroticized frame of Carlotta, hoping to attract Scottie's attention and perhaps re-ignite their once romantic relationship. Rather than transposing a visual image to a literary text, Midge transposes the image of a real self into a pictorial image, a painting. Whereas ekphrasis usually foregrounds the power of one representational system to transform or re-interpret another, Midge's prank is an attempt to inhabit the image with her own self, ironically calling attention to its ekphrastic action and underlining the dramatic difference between an erotic imaginary and the social real. Scottie, however, increasingly refuses to acknowledge the frames and borders of ekphrastic textualities, so that the images of Madeleine/Carlotta/Judy can merge as a palimpsest through his own eyes. Midge's denotative re-inscription of herself, sadly for her, materializes the ekphrastic illusion in a manner that directly confronts and disturbs the connotative chain that drives Scottie's disturbed vision.*

Describing Cinema

In describing cinema, I am not primarily interested in the ekphrastic as a dynamic that maps and measures the exchanges, for instance, between visual images and the usually literary texts that appropriate them. Nor am I interested here in the more common questions about how films themselves describe the world through their various realist aesthetics, their different narrative strategies, their cultural and ideological underpinnings, or even their editing and framing techniques. All these are important questions within debates about description and film. My focus, however, is the critical act of description that is the foundation for the reception of films, film sequences, and film images, and the extent to which those acts of descriptive reception provide a spectrum of innovative entryways into films, while at the same time dramatizing the pleasures and complexities of an active and varied spectatorship. With some irony I suppose, I may be less interested here in the films themselves than in the linguistic and rhetorical reclamation of those films as verbal and written texts. Moreover, I intend to open that dynamic in a way that gives more-than-usual free reign to the more subjective and independent force of those descriptions. As a compliment to the provisional tentativeness of all descriptions, I am interested in bold, even creative, descriptions.

For my argument, describing cinema is thus invariably, if less obviously, about rhetoric, much in the way Adorno characterizes essay writing, where "[r]hetoric was probably never anything but thought in its adaptation to communicative language" (*Notes to Literature* 20). With this approach, I follow Lesley Stern's incisive discussion in which "[d]escription is, of course, never merely description. It is always rhetorical. . . . Films live in the world and almost inevitably open out onto other films, worlds, histories, political landscapes." For her, this kind of "[c]riticism is always more interesting if it not only describes but if it probes, evidences curiosity, is attuned to resonance." V. F. Perkins's earlier comments on the relation between critical description, rhetoric, and interpretation suggests more explicitly how descriptive rhetoric acts as a kind of interpretation based in the communication of affect (which I will return to):

No intra-textual interpretation ever is or could be a proof. Most often, it is a description of aspects of the film with suggested understandings of some of the ways they are patterned. Rhetoric is involved in developing the description so that it evokes a sense of how, seen this way, the film may affect us, or so that it invites participation in the pleasure of discovering this way in which various of the film's features hang together. But the ultimate appeal for conviction is to the reader's memory and renewed experience of the film. (4)

Like any visual image, films have innumerable qualities and ways of being rhetorically described. Yet unlike an encounter with the single still image of, for example, a photograph, with film those descriptions must struggle with the very significant addition of movement and sound, additions that exponentially ramp up the challenges of description: if description is a self-conscious "pouring of the self into the now" (Doty 23), with film that interpellation of self in language must now vascillate within the gap between descriptive stasis and the resistance of imagistic and audio movement. Years before the VHS, DVD, and digital revolutions in playback spectatorship in the 1980s and 1990s, Raymond Bellour's landmark "The Unattainable Text" provocatively pinpoints the problem of quoting and citing a cinematic text because of its fundamental movement. Although today there may be the easy ability to arrest the filmic text through those technologies, the real-time experience of the text has not fundamentally altered, and significant challenges remain in trying to linguistically inhabit visually and audially mobile spaces. More recently, Laura Mulvey coincidentally retrieves the words of Woolrich's Jeffries when she characterizes a critical viewer's encounter with fragments of a film that too quickly flicker by us: this becomes an effort in which film quotation "delays" the film image, a delay she defines as "the essential process behind textual analysis." For her, the analytical opportunity in "delaying the image, extracting it from its narrative surroundings, also allows it to return to its context and to contribute something extra and unexpected, a deferred meaning, to the story's narration" (144). This in turn helps explicate the "range of looking relations" elicited by film quotation.

There are many situations and platforms through which film description occurs, contexts that necessarily shape and alter the dynamics and delays of description. Besides the fundamental act of critical writing itself, some of the most prominent and distinctive variations on description as writing include conversations, lectures, and video-essays, each with their own rebalancing of the rhetoric of description. With conversations, describing cinema usually becomes a more dialogic and interactive texture through which the description often calls attention to the gaps of memory that can also blur precise compositional details, often in the service of arguments. Here the frequent back and forth of a conversation attests especially to the challenge to accurately cite texts or even plot details, as well as to the socially productive exchanges between interlocutors that underpin all efforts to describe recently observed films. Academic lectures often—too often in my opinion—tend to minimize the dialogic shape of description and replace it with a more authoritative, almost legalistic position where description becomes evidence and proof. Video-essays usually shift the place of linguistic rhetoric from the center of description to the margins of the images being re-presented and can thus take the form of a palimpsestic reappropriation of images and sounds within a different conceptual framework. In the best of these video-essays, the rhetoric of description shifts between oral or written language and the visual syntax of the video. Yet, with some irony, the presumed textual accuracy of these video essays signals, for Erika Balsom in her superb book *Ten Skies*, the importance and power of the language of description. Repositioning Bellour's argument, she notes, "No writing will ever master, ever exhaust, the film it chases after. Neither will any piece of videographic criticism. But unlike the latter, which sublimates the cinematic experience, grabbing at bits of film, carving it up into tender morsels, writing leaves the film whole, unscathed. It hovers nearby without touching" (45). Written descriptions about film attempt "to grasp the ungraspable but never fully can, producing an imperfect translation from one medium to another. . . . Descriptions of films rebound back, hitting the films described, changing our understanding" (53).[3]

As these examples suggest, there are also numerous technical and exhibition modalities that come into play in a descriptive engagement with cinema. There is, for instance, a significant difference between the need to describe a film as an immediate and singular experience and the ability to see and re-see an image or sequence (again, enabled particularly by the viewing technologies of the last forty years). Less obviously, perhaps, are the possibilities and the limits for the description of films engaged through immersive screens, home screens, or portable screens, each of these offering different spectatorial positions that generate less or more of the distance that allows for less or more descriptive activity. Arguably, an immersive viewing experience tends to resist description or at least to shift the focus of that description from what happens on and through the screen to the visceral and kinetic experience of the viewer, while the manipulatable screens of computers and other personal digital devices allow relatively precise attention to images but sacrifice other important dimensions of the film (such as the scale and impact of large-screen images). Although these distinctions are much too schematic, they call proper attention, I believe, to how cinematic description responds invariably to the technological and social contexts that inform any descriptive encounter.

Throughout the history of cinema itself, there are likewise precedents and oblique variations on the challenges of describing film images as part of the movie experience. Films in the first decades of the twentieth century offer some of the most fundamental but often quite sophisticated precedents in their use of linguistic intertitles to provide dialogue, narrative transitions, humor, and occasionally commentary or poetic reflections on the action. Most famously perhaps is an intertitle from D. W. Griffith's

---

[3] Thanks to Anat Dan for bringing this book to my attention.

Intolerance (1916): without any direct reference to the different plots in the film, a repeated line from Walt Whitman's *Leaves of Grass*, "Out of the cradle endlessly rocking," appears as a metaphoric and connotative description of the historical repetitions that connect the four stories of the film. Within this tradition, one of the most demanding descriptive practices appears as a modern crisis that represents a struggle with the cinematic task of describing the unseen, the unseeable, or realities beyond the powers of language: the voice-over of Jean Caryol's text in the 1955 *Night and Fog* largely relinquishes both words and images of the Holocaust camps since "[t]here is no use even describing what went on here." A more recent and ambitious version of this fraught relationship between film images and verbal description is Naomi Kawase's 2017 *Radiance* in which a character (Misako) writes scripts that describe the details of films for blind or semi-blind viewer-listeners, most especially for an almost blind and highly critical photographer (Nakamori), who would then be able to hear the visuals of the film. A key comment that "[n]othing is more beautiful than that which disappears before our eyes" crystallizes the heart of the film, which is implicitly counterpointed by the realization that there may be nothing more difficult and challenging than to describe those disappearing images.[4] Then there is the stunningly vertiginous commentary in Nathalie Léger's 2012 *Suite for Barbara Loden*, about Loden's 1970 film *Wanda*, a writing exercise commissioned as a short encyclopedia entry meant "[t]o describe and only describe" the film and filmmaker but is ultimately foiled, stretched, and layered across multiple histories and personal experiences as a remarkable meditation on "a state of disorder and imperfection, its incompleteness predictable and its unfinished state programmed" (18).

---

[4] One of the more intriguing and unique variations on those descriptive intertitles appears in the tradition of the Japanese *benshii*, in which a live commentator accompanies the projection of the film, describing, narrating, and sometimes interpreting the film images. Notably, the same film might, at another screening, elicit different descriptions or comments from the same *benshii*.

The challenges and subsequent energy of cinematic description shift grounds—especially after World War II and the 1940s, a historical watershed period for my argument—when the encounter between the cinema and a descriptive language moves outside the films themselves and begins to charge and shape, more subjectively, critical writing and reviews about movies. In *The Rhapsodes: How 1940s Critics Changed American Film Culture*, David Bordwell has argued, for instance, that the 1940s represented significant shifts in the rhetorical power of film criticism, specifically in the writings of Otis Ferguson, Parker Tyler, Many Farber, and James Agee, where their essays invigorated movie criticism with a fresh intelligence and creative rhetoric that would reverberate into the twenty-first century. With Agee, Bordwell notes, his "frank subjectivity in the *Nation* pieces yielded a bracing sense of an actual person talking to you. Instead of supplying a fixed assessment, he dramatized the act of wrestling out a provisional sense of the film's accomplishment. . . . [H]is rhetoric projected an exquisite sensibility trying to do justice to each film at hand, to his immediate experience of it, and to the experience as recollected in (relative) tranquility" (73). Saliently or obliquely, I'd argue, some of the most engaging and perceptive film criticism since then has followed this path where the incorporation of creative description becomes the foundation for critical insight, a tradition and practice with which I align my argument here.

It is almost commonplace to say that Vertigo *describes itself: as an elaborately self-conscious and reflexive engagement with the essential cinematic compositions that are at the thematic center of its story: visions, images, and frames. Yet, it also describes itself as a film about the difficulty, if not impossibility, of adequately and clearly describing its tortured visual world with a denotative visual and aural language. Galvin Elster's bromidic description of his wife's peculiar behavior early in the film, the linguistic flatness of Scottie's trial, or the gabby Midge's formulaic attempt to resuscitate the emotionally crippled Scottie, all appear as if superfluous interventions in a film whose most dramatic moments are almost silent, focused frequently on the dumbfounded and sometime catatonic Scottie. Descriptive language flounders throughout* Vertigo, *as silence overwhelms so many of its central sequences, as an inarticulable emptiness made more vibrant by Bernhard Hermann's swaying underscore. When Scottie follows Madeleine to a museum gallery, the immensely rich visual movements—with zooms and pans darting between his eyes and the coiffed hair and bouquets that link Madeleine and the portrait of Carlotta—seem almost beyond or before words in a sequence. Throughout the film, adrift in the spinning anxiety of a musical score, language appears too late to account for the action and almost irrelevant to the vertiginous spaces. Does the final silent image of Scottie peering down at another abstract body gaspingly refuse, resist, or at least deflect linguistic description?*

This difficulty of articulating and describing a world of elusive images persists today, provoking and generating, I would argue, a subtle anxiety, or at least urgency, in the description of films. Based in a somewhat open-ended—and in an important sense, a more or less arbitrary process—that moves beyond the mechanisms of those traditional cornerstones of cinematic identification and cognition, describing cinema today has become a pervasive and fluctuating rhetorical and hermeneutical action at the center of the film experience, spread across the spate of fluent reviews, lively blogs, and stylish academic writing about film. Across the proliferation (and underlying anxiety) of so much contemporary critical activity, the exuberant possibility of the *arbitrary*, as the sign of a constantly fluctuating critical subjectivity, measures, I believe, the energy of an asystematic encounter with a cinematic world of whatever.

Affective Description

As a measure of the productive and often creative range of cinematic descriptions, this open provocation to describe aligns, most notably, with the wide range of cinematic affects. Just as a vague "disturbance" in his "subconscious" (83) provokes and elicits Woolrich's Jeffries's descriptive investigation of the moving frames across from his apartment, acts of describing cinema are, perhaps needless to say, always motivated. More varied than Jeffries's motivations, however, cinematic descriptions respond to a shifting play of affects as they commonly follow sometimes singular, sometimes overlapping, affective encounters.

The contemporary interest in affect theory and practice has produced an array of definitions and investigations, exploring affect as a field of communicative intensities, pre-subjective emotions, and physical responses. In their introduction to *The Affect Theory Reader*, "An Inventory of Shimmers," Gregory J. Seigworth and Melissa Gregg delineate for me an affective grounding of that gray zone of cinematic description, where an affective "duration" recalls both Jefferies's and Mulvey's "delayed action":

> Affect arises *in-between-ness*: in the capacities to act and be acted on. Affect is an impingement or extrusion of a momentary or sometimes more sustained state of relation *as well as* the passage (and the duration of passage) of forces and intensities. . . . [It] can serve to drive us toward movement, toward thought and extension, that can likewise suspend us (as if in neutral) across a barely registering accretion of force-relations or that can even leave us overwhelmed by the world's apparent intractability. (1)

Like other critical investigations that explore the circulation of these "forces and intensities" in various anthropological or public realms, the place of these affects seems, following Deleuze's pre-linguistic placement of it, to inhabit a blurred space that precedes or evades specific articulation. In contrast, Eugenie Brinkema's study *The Forms of Affect* locates the force and movement of affect precisely in its formal articulation. Affect "invokes force more than transmission, a force that does not have to move from subject to object but may fold back, rebound, recursively amplify . . . the double bind of affect—action or the capacity to be acted on, which leaves open the lively and forceful dimension of the word without reducing it to a transference between agents—and interior states, such as mood, feeling, or desire, which is the sense in which it has been evoked most often in the history of philosophy" (24). According to Brinkema, most models of affect in the humanities focus on affect's power to "disrupt, interrupt, reinsert, demand, provoke, insist on, remind of, agitate for," yet those models tend to characterize affect as a mostly abstract force that, to some extent, deflates the concept, leaving "only the mild rhetorical force of summary and paraphrase, intoned synonyms, and thematic generalizations" (xii, xiii). Instead, she insists: "*Affect is not the place where something immediate and automatic and resistant takes place outside of language. The turning to affect in the humanities does not obliterate the problem of form and representation*" (xiv, author's emphasis). Through the vehicles of forms, representations, and language, "The one way out for affect is via a way into its specificities" that are part of a shared formal configuration (xiv). Accordingly, and most suggestive for my position, the "insistence on the formal dimension of affect allows not only for specificity but for the wild and many fecundities of specificity: difference, change, the particular, the contingent (*and*) the essential, the definite, the distinct, all dense details, and—again, to return to the spirit of Deleuze—the minor, inconsequential, secret, atomic" (xv). Affects are, in short, produced and reproduced by specific representations and linguistic particulars.

While for Brinkema those representational vehicles appear in the formal specificities of a film, I shift the re-articulation or double articulation of those specificities to the viewer-speaker-writer as a communication with a viewer-listener-reader. In the actions of describing cinema as a subjective encounter attempting to communicate a potentially shared insight and experience, the distinctions and specificities of affect become the distinctions and specificities of a rhetoric of representations put in play by the critical act of describing the multiple affects of film images. Importantly, this figuration of affect includes the movement and play of thought and after-thought—a spectrum of intellectual and conceptual experiences gleaned from other films and other writings—assimilated and provoked within the descriptive rhetoric of representations. For my project here, that play of thought and after-thought often emerges in the interruptions and extensions by pertinent reminders of scholarly or theoretical positions that inflect the flow of the cinematic descriptions. To describe is also, inevitably, productively to call sometimes on the history of a viewer's thinking about film and other disciplines.

Among a potentially long list of specific descriptive affects is a multiplicity of filmic provocations. Some more broadly resonant than others, they can include disturbances, bewilderments, enticements, disgusts, confusions, shocks, longings, and excitements, and, given the commercial logic of narrative filmmaking, it is no surprise that these provocations frequently stand out at the beginnings and conclusions of films, which for mainstream movies especially serve as flashpoints and enticements for viewer responses. Wherever these affects appear in a film, however, they can provoke and solicit a range of particular and precise affective positions in a cinematic description, re-activating those images and sounds according to different rhetorical strategies or configurations. As the central circuit in a descriptive exchange, a film sequence might be subject to the rhetoric of selection, amplification, eroticization, puzzlement, and, less obviously and more complexly, reviewing and layering (to name a few). In a critical sense, these acts of descriptions—as speech or writing—appropriate and extend particular affects as a way to measure, to neutralize, or to re-invigorate them as more or less precise or imprecise rhetorical engagements for which, in this project, I use a single word as a conceptual flag that identifies that particularity in each film for me.

My description of the tensely rapid "Waterloo Station" sequence in *The Bourne Ultimatum* (2007), for instance, positions me between the quick and shifting perspectives of different computer and surveillance screens layered in and across the film images and the flight of Jason Bourne, captured by those images, in a way that mimics the rhetoric of a video game or "gaming," a rhetorical recreation of various suspenseful affects and velocities which is in effect and in delay a textured interpretation of that specific sequence. Other critical positions may motivate different descriptions of this sequence, yet even the most denotative description will invariably, if less prominently, signal an interpretive action and position.

To a certain extent, it would be possible to catalogue or prioritize these kinds of affects across the history of film genres, specific textual practices, and different viewer relationships with films. Here, though, I am more interested in differentiating and detailing the rhetorical productions that emerge within these affective descriptions than in (impossibly) listing a full spectrum of them. As Brinkema suggests, the true force of affect lies in providing the concrete details and formal differences that, for me, appear in the detailed description generated by or released in writing.

One of the most common forms of describing cinema is, I should add, what I call an after-affects description. These are descriptions based in efforts to recount film narratives, and they typically follow or expand upon an initial affective engagement: how we describe a story may spring from how certain details or dimensions of the film affected us or not as part of the texture of numerous primary or preliminary affects.[5] Thus, an after-affect of my response to the Waterloo Station sequence in *The Bourne Ultimatum* (as well as other sequences in the film) describes the narrative of

---

[5] From a different angle, Georg Lukacs discusses this distinction in the 1930s in his evaluation of the two different tactics for literary narration, "Narrate or Describe?" Contrasting Tolstoy and Zola, Lukacs opposes an immersive "experience" of a narrative with the mere "observation" of information offered by description (116), since, for Lukacs the complexity of narrative immersion and interaction "establishes proportions," while "description merely levels" the density of historical experience as surface images (127). While Lukacs's polemic makes sense in the context of its ideological underpinnings (differentiating novelistic strategies), shifting his argument to acts of cinematic reception fundamentally dissolves his dichotomy and relocates it as an affective blending.

that film this way: as a tale of a man entrapped in a universe of technologies in which to survive the anonymity of his image (and retrieve a lost identity) requires mastery of those technologies as relentless and remarkable feats of execution. To recount parts or the whole of a film narrative usually becomes a descriptive encounter motivated by different degrees of attention, awareness, or interest based in, for example, an initial fascination, confusion, or boredom with specific parts of that narration or even specific images or sounds. That interest and awareness then meld dramatic actions, salient events, visual details, and audial materials positions in a far less predictable manner than conventional cognitive responses to narrative structures and movements suggest.[6] Depending on the level of attention or awareness, in short, describing a film narrative involves a more or less intricately entwined balance between compositional details and narrative actions, a selective process through which viewers necessarily narrate their own positions within the movement of the story. Attentive descriptions of a film narrative can vary considerably, not simply according to which elements of plot and action anchor the description. More significantly, these descriptions will vary according to the extent to which those particular narrative movements galvanize different visual or audial details embedded in those narrative actions. To tell the story of a film, the most engaged descriptions will gather the descriptive details around the action as an interpretive embedding of the facts of that story but not necessarily the conclusive meaning of that story.

---

[6] In *The World Viewed*, Stanley Cavell anticipated my position here in his attention to the productive unreliability of our memories of film which he called "[s]elf-confident errors," a stance I regrettably criticized in 1980 (xi). "A reading, like any recitation," he notes, "is by all means to be checked for its accuracy," but these readings involve "the reciprocity between element and significance" that he calls "the cinematic circle" (xiii-xiv). Within this circle, there is " 'the immediate and tremendous burden' on one's capacity for critical description in accounting for one's experience of film" (xiv).

Vertiginous Description

Seventy-five years after Woolrich's story was published and sixty-three years after *Rear Window* adapted it, one sequence in Hitchcock's 1958 *Vertigo* still haunts me across a spectrum of singular affects swirling around each other. With its social circumference in the 1950s, moving through postwar gender turbulence, the emergence of art cinema, and widescreen (Vista Vision) technology, *Vertigo* twists and turns through frames of auteurism and a melodramatic thriller to reshape Jeffries as an older and dizzier Scottie within a *mise-en-abyme* of counter-punctual tracks and zooms, now unwittingly inhabiting what William Rothman's calls Hitchcock's "murderous gaze." Like other Hitchcock films, in *Vertigo* description always begins with the drama of looking and listening, both of which require an attention that can too easily slip into the danger of distraction, the danger of the details, of vibrant flowers, of hairstyles, of city streets, of jeweled pendants. Might distraction here be the counterpart of the classical gaze? With too much attention or too much distraction, loss—in the story and in the viewing experience—pulls the protagonists and viewers alike out of the narrative. This may be the fundamental challenge of describing cinema. As many have pointed out, it is also the dynamic that makes *Vertigo* such a quintessential arena for description and its essential relationship to the pleasures of desire and the dangers of belatedness. As Scottie discovers amidst his trauma of seeing and re-seeing, as a darker version of the immobile Jefferies's "delayed action," describing cinema is always, like re-inscribing and remaking lost images, "too late."

Early in the film, Scottie trails Madeleine, a ghostly figure presumably possessed by a past that leads her to a church graveyard and later a museum gallery, alternately places of physical death and imagistic resurrection. Bridging and suturing these scenes is a sequence in a flower shop. From the start of the sequence, the face and expression of Jimmy Stewart is that of a star in trouble with his role—as a traumatized detective, a wandering lover, a haunted exorcist, a Hollywood embodiment of a wonderful life, a former photo journalist—whose eyes search nervously, fearfully as he steers through the vertical highs and lows of San Francisco streets, the twisting hard turns, vertiginous recollections, protected but also blinded by a windshield frame that internally masks the world he pursues and then becomes the lens of obsession. The eyes, the facial expression, and the frame are a frame and perspective that longs to stop or solve the mysteries of the world (as the photographer Jefferies once could), to arrest its relentless and fugitive movement, as an impossible moment of description, a hopeless effort not to be "too late." But, looking back from my place as a viewer of the film, the car, the clothing, the fashions are already "too late," markers of another time, a 1950s America permeated by other stressed traumas and other stressed sexualities. Looking back from 2023, this too is time travel, like the layered voices and views from Chris Marker's 1982 Sunless, *a distracted detour at one point into the world of* Vertigo.

Twenty minutes into the film, Scottie, whose desperately troubled eyes are only intensified by that shielding frame of a windshield follows Madeleine's exotically and morbidly green and luxurious car into a dark back alley. (Why is she using the backdoor of the shop, I wonder? What is wrong here?) A virtually silent scene except for the almost sickly dreamy score of Bernard Herrmann. Why this backway, this shadowy tunnel? An entry to some dangerous back room, the back room of consciousness? The underbelly of desire? I go back to the opening sequence: the dark ellipsis between death and guilt. An antechamber of garbage cans and brooms leading toward yet another shadowy doorway, overwhelming Scottie's dull and proper hat, suit, and tie, not unlike Madeleine's proper gray suit and tightly coiffed hair that barely conceals the spiral that mesmerizes and disturbs beneath the propriety. The shot/counter-shot and track of Scottie's searching look, a belated and delayed shot through the alley as an always following vision, the double entendre of this following shot, always behind, always too late to grasp with words.

Then the slow wipe from left to right as Scottie opens the opaque door like a slide that becomes the palimpsestic opening of his sight as mind. The Technicolor excess of brilliant flowers—purples, pinks, and yellows, gladiolas, and roses amidst which Madeleine wanders nonchalantly, middle grounded against the prosaic movement of other customers in the background. A claustrophobia and entombment within the image: the luxury of being dead. A saleswoman approaches, briefly speaks with Madeleine, and then retreats to retrieve her bouquet. Madeleine wanders, eyes right in a slightly nervous or self-conscious or performative way—toward Scottie's position peeping through the door. How can she not notice him peering through the crack in the door? Then the shot, the key shot, a key-hole shot into a descriptive mise-en-abyme: *an image split by Madeleine's reflection in the door's multiple mirrors on the left and the dark sliver of open doorway on the right through which one eye is visible, an eye buried in darkness, an eye unable to see with the depth of stereoscopic sight. She looks down to the left, before a cut to his one eye straight at her and at us. (Did Scottie's police partner look him in the eye before he fell?) Their eyelines parallel each other at the same level of the frame. The figure of Madeleine becomes fantastically broken, shattered by the edges of smaller mirrors on that border of the door mirror that captures and describes her. This is an image that ricochets toward us and then back to her and then back to him, swirling like a forward dolly and reverse zoom, the renowned Vertigo effect. She looks up to her right, deliberately exhibiting a face in profile and, after a cut, turns her back, and looks down right, offering the other flattened profile. The inquisitive, threatened, and longing look and the exhibitionistic, taunting pose balanced within the frame for us as a tension between a concentrated, enhanced look and spinning, paralyzing distractions. Why have I no place across their eyelines that match only as a confrontation and disruption. I know you're looking at me from the movement of your face. The woman arrives with the bouquet for Carlotta.*

Here to see is to be lost in the spinning frame of a resisting image that ultimately begs for some kind of descriptive stoppage like the desperate framing of desire. But this is a description that is never quite achievable with the moving images of the cinema. That impossible stoppage requires the work of a re-inscription, a re-inscription that later becomes, for Scottie in this film, a twisted makeover and reinvention of a lost image, of Judy as Madeleine as Carlotta—an embedded emblem of the endless activity that is cinematic description.

My Furtive Glance

A series of short rhetorical snapshots of celebrated paintings and photographs, Jean-Luc Nancy and Federico Ferrari's book, *Being Nude*, is one of my models for the energy of verbal description as it engages the visual.[7] Indeed, the short reflections or meditations on a series of paintings and photographs of nude figures proceed in a way that anticipates some of my own method for describing specific sequences in film history as underpinned by a kind of "arbitrariness and chance," which is less of an approach than "a flaneur's wandering," awakened by "some movement of curiosity or desire, but is never reduced to it." In this way, as perhaps in the way *Vertigo* spins the challenges of describing cinema back into a place within the history of art, within a history of Western art in which "the repeated attempt of a furtive glance—peering through a window (as in Renaissance art, for example) or leaning over the lens of a camera obscura (as in seventeenth-century Dutch art)"—becomes an attempt "to grasp a subject who is more or less aware of being observed." As a result, "The image does not close over; it fails to come to a standstill or to insist on a particular whole. The eye is set in motion" (2-3, 31, 33). So, I would argue, is a visibly mobile language where the dynamics of words or a single word can become an expansive view finder into one of the many centers of a film.

---

[7] Thanks to Eugenie Brinkema for recommending this book.

PART II

"BADLY SAID, BADLY SEEN"

1

Describing . . . Dis-chord: *Meet Me in St. Louis* (Vincente Minnelli, 1944)

André Bazin famously distinguished theater from cinema by describing the difference between a world lit by a chandelier and a world explored with a flashlight. Released just seven years before Bazin's two-part essay on "Theater and Cinema" and notably not adapted from a theatrical drama, *Meet Me in St. Louis* nonetheless strikes me as a movie about a theatrical world disrupted by a flashlight perspective that continually threatens to trouble those dramatic spaces and players, as that shaky light explores the stages and corners of those places and characters. Of the many potential delights and complexities in this film, one that especially engages me is how the

Describing Cinema. Timothy Corrigan, Oxford University Press. © Oxford University Press 2024.
DOI: 10.1093/oso/9780197625354.003.0002

film counterpoints its magnificent chandelier celebrations in a grand Victorian home and the impending World's Fair with the discordant shadows and dark shades that it exposes on the edges of those two Technicolor spectacles, those shadows and shades regularly threatening to dim or extinguished those mesmerizing light shows. Think of those angrily auspicious shadows dancing around the Halloween bonfires of burning furniture that pursue Tootie to the trolley tracks that night; think of perhaps the most forlorn Christmas melody ever performed on the December eve, a melody, with such unexpectedly somber counter chords, about losing a family home and all its supposedly harmonious stability.

For instance and later, the conclusion of the film climaxes with grandiose theatrics when the family gathers to watch the light show of the 1904 World's Fair in St. Louis, a town in mid-America that was in reality emerging, like so many American and world cities, from the darkness of 1944 and World War II, but in the film's narrative has been returned through an extended flashback to 1903–1904, crystallizing a utopian nostalgia in which St. Louis appears as the beginnings of a vibrant twentieth-century America. During my first viewings of this movie many years ago, I was struck during this climactic scene by the almost incidental appearance of two Catholic nuns—no doubt an unusual observation and fixation produced by my long-ago Catholic heritage—strolling conspicuously (for me) across that crowded scene that then closes around Tootie, Esther, and the entire Smith family. Now, I think this moment, punctuated by those figures of piety, sin, and repentance, retroactively might suggest to a viewer—or at least this viewer—several markers in the film that, spread across the Technicolor energy and optimism of the movie, gesture toward the muted Christian tale underpinning *Meet Me in St. Louis,* a tale not just about the celebration of family but also about the discord, loss, and violence counterpointing so many upbeat songs and sing-alongs, family harmonies, and lavish costumes, a discord that resonates outside the film frames toward the historical and moral darkness of the struggling humanity of the

1940s, in the violent shadows of World War II, in the fading lights of a post-Enlightenment world where the fracturing of a dominant patriarchal power has begun to undo the ideological sanctity of the family that traditional society has always feigned to defend. From this angle, *Meet Me in St. Louis* is for me, to be blunt, a horror film breaking the surface of Richard Dyer's utopian narrative that defines so many Hollywood musicals. While delighted viewers embrace throughout the film the ebullient harmonies of an anxious trolley song or the romantic but uneasy rhythmic longings for "the boy next door," I hear strained chords and lyrics that make this film far more unsettling and difficult to describe.

Beginning with silly arguments about the taste of ketchup, the shadows of discord begin to emerge immediately from the unlit corners of this family romance and its glittering surfaces: there are the anxious deceptions about Rose's romantic telephone call in order to deviously dismiss a clueless father, and later a shocked and rattled family accuses and then attacks that boy next door, John Truett, after a supposed assault on Tootie, the youngest sister. The dark night of Halloween, the eve of the dead, releases, however, the most troubling cacophony of harsh notes, associated, again, with Tootie, whose obsession with death, dead dolls, and burials contrasts—hilariously? horrifically?—with the childish innocence of her age. The almost chaotic Halloween sequence then draws out a tongue-in-cheek atmosphere of violence and disorder, as costumed children roam the neighborhood and Tootie successfully completes her mission to symbolically "murder" an elderly neighbor by assaulting him with what she hopes will be a deadly handful of flour.

Toward the end of the film, this dissonant bass line for the music of family erupts when Tootie metaphorically bludgeons the snowpeople replicants of her own family. For me, the brutality of this sequence becomes a different clanging—so much different from that of the trolley full of young romantics—that can barely be recuperated by a narrative almost desperately bent on integrating disruption into happy family melodies.

Shortly after the posturing patriarch Mr. Smith has summarily decided and announced that the family will move from St. Louis to a dystopian New York City, the sequence begins in a darkened, nighttime bedroom where a medium close-up of Tootie and her sister Esther becomes the stage for their strained duet of "Have Yourself a Merry, Little Christmas," a tune meant to comfort but here teeters and gasps as a mournful rendition in which there is little merriment. Even seemingly optimistic verses ring hollow, and it was no surprise when I discovered that the lyrics in the film barely paper over the original, much gloomier words of songwriter Ralph Blane: while Esther mournfully sings, "Next year all our troubles will be far away . . . Faithful friends who were dear to us will be near to us once more" they barely repress the original lyrics that Judy Garland found, ironically, too gloomy: "Next year we may all be many miles away," Blane had written, "Faithful friends who were dear to us will be near to us no more" (Kaufman 9). This might indeed be a very "little" Christmas, with friends and families separated by growing global instabilities and movements, unrecoverable losses of those friends and families, and warm lights growing dimmer.

When, at the start of the sequence, Esther enters Tootie's moonlit bedroom on Christmas eve, the two gaze out the window across at John Truett's window, where he stands clearly troubled by the unspoken complications in his marriage proposal to Esther as she is about to be vanquished to New York. He pulls down a shade, darkening the window frame through which Esther and Tootie had been watching him, so that a spider web of tree branches crosses the surface of the window. In a medium two-shot, Tootie explains that she will take all her dolls, "even the dead ones," to New York City. When Esther explains she can bring all her dolls with her, "except of the snow people of course," Tootie giggles uneasily and a reverse long shot reveals the cluster of a carefully arranged family of snow men and women in a dark bluish light. In a hardly comforting comment, Esther notes, "we'd look pretty silly trying to get them on the train." She then begins the song, accompanied by a music box of toy mechanical monkeys in the close-up space between the two sisters, a more disturbing than cute reminder of the other-than-human shapes and energies that percuss through the body of the narrative and world beyond St. Louis. Esther's radiant extreme close-up with teary eyes looking upward contrasts with Tootie's downward look and tear-stained cheeks.

Overwhelmed by the melancholy of the situation, Tootie rushes out of the room, past the always confused father on a barren staircase marked by the ghostly outlines of picture frames now removed, to the yard below where she has, in happier times, built that family of snow people, icy models her own increasingly icy family. As the now more urgent and rising chords of Esther's tune follow her, a weeping Tootie begins to smash the heads and bodies of the snow people dressed in hats and accessories to resemble her proper family. She first beheads and then breaks apart the body of the stand-in for her brother, before beating off the heads of the father and mother and bludgeoning, with a remarkable ferocity, a small snow creature that begins to crumble under the blows. When Esther arrives to stop her, Tootie sobs through echoes of desperation, "Nobody's goin' to have them if we have to go to New York. I'd rather kill them!" So much for family, so much for innocence.

Next is a cut to a close-up of the concerned father witnessing the scene from an upper-story window in the house, followed by a point-of-view shot of Tootie in the yard now joined by Esther who continues her failing efforts to comfort her weeping sister: "New York is a wonderful town . . . . Everyone dreams about going there," she pleads weakly and unconvincingly. "We're luckier than lots of families because we're actually going! . . . The friends we'll make . . ." A reverse shot of the meditative father in the window marks the revelation of the scene for him, a man passive and befuddled throughout the film, as most males in the film also appear, almost paralyzed before the emotions and actions of the women whose musical control of this place has faded into sobs. Above Tootie's loud moans, the emptiness of Esther's shaky, hardly heard, and bromidic commonplaces about New York barely signify or comfort Tootie before her graphic destruction of a fantasy family, a family so white and fragile that, if not battered and beheaded, they would certainly soon melt like Dorothy's wicked witch five years earlier. In a two-shot of Esther kneeling before Tootie, punctuated with a reverse shot of Mr. Smith in the upstairs window, Esther pleads, as much to her own unbelieving self as to Tootie, "the main thing, Tootie, is that we're all going to be together, just as we've always been. We can be anywhere as long as we're together." As she hugs the weeping Tootie, this attempted comfort rings, for me, as hopelessly flat, off-key, and dissonant for a family so fully enmeshed in their grand home and vibrant hometown that to be uprooted and displaced from them will, presumably, offer nothing but claustrophobic kitchens and noisy streets. For this family, I am now convinced, there can be no togetherness or happiness outside the parameters of St. Louis. On the edges or in the backyards of these homes, for this former Dorothy, there is, desperately, hysterically, now more than ever, "no place like it," where, in the wake of their potential displacement, the songs of a trolley car would become the screeching of wheels and discordant clanging of that same trolley and where the boy next door could potentially become a predator. 1944 is not 1939, and that prewar Kansas home threatens to become no home in a 1944 Missouri.

The now meditative father slowly lowers the window and crosses from that windowsill into the dark room, the room now barely lit by the moon illuminating a prone doll in the foreground. He walks through the room and lifts one of the dolls of a lost childhood, deep in thought. The now awakened other sister, Agnes, sleepily asks, "What's the matter, papa?" As he covers her with the blankets on her bed, he quietly calms himself and murmurs, with a low ironic tone, "Everything's fine." He exists the room, closing the door, looks at his pocket watch (is it too late to go back in time like the flashback that structures the film?), then looks at the wall marked by those numerous outlines of missing picture frames and vacated images as he descends into the darkened foyer below. This grand Victorian home possessed—culturally, historically, existentially— by change and loss is now a haunted house, a dispossessed household with doors and windows that are now open to those hostile streets of Halloween. The ghosts of movement and change, I realize, have become the almost inconceivable threat to life, family, and comfort. This may be a cinematic version of what Una Chaudhuri has labelled "geopathology," where the "problem of place—and place as problem" now have begun to appear "as a series of ruptures and displacements, from the micro- to the macrospatial, from home to nature, with intermediary space concepts such as neighborhood, hometown, community, and country ranged in between" (55). A chorus of discordant places in the heart of the heart of the country where, at this notable historical and cultural watershed of the 1940s, the celebrations of the utopian musicals begin to change registers through the anxious voices and spaces of movie melodramas that begin to open out to the unknown horizons and instabilities of the road movie. For Esther, Tootie and the entire family are about to hit the open road.

Deep in thought within the mounting registers and higher musical chords of horns and violins, Mr. Smith surveys the pictures on the floor and boxes and barrels packed and ready for the move, meditating as Esther carries a slumped Tootie across the back of the scene and up the stairs. Taking a seat and staring across the dim room filled with boxes and crates, he lights a cigar, as distant music of the theme song "Meet Me in St. Louis" slowly rises to mark his moments of a growing clarity. A tracking shot moves closer and closer to his face, as he strikes a match that gradually enlightens his face like a beam from a Bazinian flashlight. He stops as the match hovers over the cigar, and his quickly shifting eyes speak the expression of a revelation that even in this modern world, in the fading tones of musical harmony, travel and movement may not be necessary. "Anna! Anna!" he shouts to his wife and family as he gathers them to announce a change of plans. They all regroup under that theatrical chandelier, well away from those shaky beams of a cinematic flashlight.

Why, though, does this shout sound to me like a desperately shrill note from a patriarch attempting an impossible reversal of the movement off stage into a different cinematic future?

2

Describing . . . The Pedestrian:
The Bicycle Thieves
(Vittorio De Sica, 1948)

As so often, I find my beginning in André Bazin who wrote, "It would be no exaggeration to say that *Ladri de Biciclette* is the story of a walk through Rome by a father and his son. Whether the child is ahead, behind, alongside . . . what he is doing is never without meaning" ("Bicycle Thief" 55). This minimal description succinctly and accurately pinpoints the achievements and challenges of Vittoria De Sica's *Bicycle Thieves* with its minimal plot, bare and empty setting in the streets of Rome, and actors who are non-actors.

Describing Cinema. Timothy Corrigan, Oxford University Press. © Oxford University Press 2024.
DOI: 10.1093/oso/9780197625354.003.0003

Set in the economic crisis of a depressed postwar Rome, the film recounts the theft of a bicycle that a man, Antonio Ricci, needs in order to remain employed, and he and his son, Bruno, set out to search for the missing bike. They walk and walk and walk from crowded markets and unremarkable streets, desperately without certain direction. They are already the walking dead, a reality which Ricci self-consciously glimpses and introjects late in the film when the drowned body of a boy, almost his son, is pulled from the Tiber, a river named after a drowned Etruscan king, which might also remind him and the descriptive viewer that there is no real destination within the impenetrable flow of a murky river. If screenwriter Cesare Zavatini famously claimed for this and other neorealist films that they should eschew the drag and pulsion of a narrative plot in attending to the reality of the everyday, I wonder if such an attenuated narrative can simply wander without a destination, even while it struggles to fit that story within a classic narrative of the evolving bond of a father and son, pedestrians with no obvious destination in world of pedestrian objects and events, pursuing the phantoms of lost bicycles. A double-edged (s)word for *The Bicycle Thieves*: the pedestrian as a mode of walking, the pedestrian as the non-event of the everyday.

Without forward mobility, to seek is to wander with uncertain steps. How appropriate that the theft occurs while Ricci works to plaster a poster of Rita Hayworth in the 1946 *Gilda* on a street wall since the loss of his bike in this sequence signals also the loss of a classical cinematic tradition in which driving action, spectacular costumes and sets, and intense melodramatic emotions could propel characters and their plots. For some, that world of progressive action has become a memory in postwar Europe. (What, I wonder, might it mean that decades later, in 1994, a similar life-size poster of Hayworth reappears in the *Shawshank Redemption*, where it is one of the posters that covers a hole in a cell wall, through which the falsely accused Andy escapes a corrupt prison and crawls through the waste in a sewer line. The lost image of a lost mobility historically reappears here at the entrance to a desperate crawl space leading back to the Hollywood beach fantasy that ends that film. Today, I guess, we need to crawl before we can walk, let alone ride, back to that Hollywood narrative.)

A digression: In his monumental studies *Cinema 1* and *Cinema 2*, Gilles Deleuze notes the centrality of filmic description within the Italian neorealism films of the 1940s, including *The Bicycle Thieves*, and later in the French New Wave cinema, at one point comparing the work of Jacques Rivette and Jean-Luc Godard where "description tends toward a point of indiscernibility of the real and the imaginary" (2, 12). For Deleuze, the prominence of a descriptive cinema in these postwar decades is a product of the watershed shift in the 1940s when "a cinema of seeing replaces action" (9), "a cinema of the seer and no longer of the agent" (2). Description across the indiscernibility of the seen by agents without agency.

In *The Bicycle Thieves*, that indiscernibility and the seer's lack of agency become the foundation for a world permeated by redundancies and accidentals that create an experiential monotony that seems to subvert the distinctions that usually empower critical description as writing—and ultimately as meaning, numbing redundancies and inimical accidentals, highlighted for me in the all-too-everyday Piazza Vittorio sequence. What this sequence— and many others in the film—describes is not simply the search for a bicycle and agency but also the fragile, changing, and perhaps doomed relationship between a father and son.

Ricci and Bruno's search begins in the weekend market of Piazza Vittorio where they are joined by Ricci's friend Baicco and his workmen. (Baicco, an old friend whom Ricci had asked for help with his desperate crisis earlier when Baicco rehearsed a local theatrical production in the back rooms of a building, where the drama of theatrics contrasts, as throughout the film, with the raw reality of the streets.) The sequence occurs early in the film after police give Ricci little hope of finding his bike in a city suffused with an economic crisis, joblessness, and rampant crime. In the

black-and-white shadows of a cobbled street, Ricci and his son arrive on a streetcar and descend near the vast marketplace—the last
time where any vehicle would offer the two any mobility, the last
time they will enjoy any mobility other than pointless walking. As
they descend into the somber street, within a medium-long shot,
the father and son move in one direction and then quickly correct
themselves and turn to move quickly the opposite direction, direction and location already a difficult decision, as the small son
jogs to keep pace with the tall father, always a step behind and
crossing paths with the movements of carriages, trucks, and garbage carts pushed down the street by a phalanx of men. In those
streets crowded with men struggling to move through and around
the barricades of objects and junk, seeing replaces action, and
seeing becomes a series of restless shifts embodied in the constantly
moving eyelines of the characters.

As they begin to wander through the market, the father and
son visually rummage through the street markets overflowing
with the reusable waste of parts and leftovers, the past remains of
disassembled scrap whose use value has been suspended. The es-
sence of a pedestrian life. Asked by his friend to identify the lost
bike, Bruno quickly answers—with an irony that permeates the
film—that it is a "lightweight Fides," faith becoming more and
more lightweight with each corner turned. Ricci's quick comments
that his son "knows [the bike] better than me" is already a casual
alert, I think, that the hierarchy of the father-son relationship may
be shifting ground, beginning the gradual inversion of that conventional familial balance. In this postwar society, the traditional spiritual or social faith in the family and its traditional hierarchies has
begun to erode, just as Ricci's own faith in a better life gradually
collapses with each encounter, to be replaced, for Ricci's wife and
later for Ricci, by, at best, the bogus truisms of a local fortune-teller,
a parody of faith in a spiritual order. A lost bicycle is a lost mobility
is a lost human agency is a lost faith in human relationships and
a future whose growth and development might once have been

figured in the narrative continuity of the child as father of the man but whose bonding continuity has been fractured with each step through these labyrinthine streets of Rome.

Baicco, his fellow workers, Ricci, and Bruno then set out to search the blocks and blocks of bicycles and bicycle parts—tires, frames, and bells—for incriminating pieces of the stolen bike, scattered perhaps across a piazza market that now appears as a consumer wasteland. The group walks through the dim morning streets toward the market, again changing directions suddenly to reorient within the continual disorientation in these streets, their hope to reconstruct that lost Fides "piece by piece" already exacerbated by a perspective moving corporeally at ground level, without a larger overview. As the market opens and vendors begin to display their bikes and parts, the group walks past racks of tires and tables of parts, before Bruno is sent off by himself to inspect "pumps and bells," a rare separation of father and son. Despite Ricci's promise to celebrate together when they find the lost bike, this separation is casually foreboding of the growing rift between these two anxious pedestrians, father and son, surrounded by the detritus of a capitalist consumer culture left on the streets of a postwar society.

A slow horizontal shot tracks Bruno as he inspects bicycle parts in the stalls. As the vendors brush him aside brusquely ("beat it, kid"), he turns back to his father and in a medium shot he clutches Ricci, eyes turned adoringly, desperately upward at the chagrined, searching eyes of the father. The group of men then huddle around Bruno and begin slowly walking down the covered passageway; in a hardly noticeable background of the shot appears part of a magazine stand with covers featuring glamorous women, recalling for an instant that climactic and disastrous moment when Ricci pastes the fantasy of a movie poster on a wall just prior to the theft of his bicycle. Traditional masculinity and conventional Hollywood glamour are gratingly out of place here. Or perhaps it is Ricci who has lost his place here among the lingering relics of another world?

As multiple bicycles are wheeled out before them, Bruno's eyes hardly glance at the bike but remain continually fixed upward on the face of his father—watching anxiously for paternal wisdom or assurance?—as they wander, randomly, slowly and cautiously, through the market, searching the stalls and racks of a crowded urban jungle of bickering and defensive vendors. Arguments erupt in a marketplace that reeks of hostile capitalism, within which this almost comic band of well-meaning misfits, inspecting bikes, almost clinging together in defense, stands no chance. A close-up tracks from right to left across the handlebars of a row of bicycles, a repetition that gradually disperses any specific identification into repeated rows of sameness (already anticipated in the earlier sequence in which a shot shows Ricci and his wife's hocked wedding linens stored on shelf upon shelf upon shelf of other hocked linens). A tracking shot, from right to left cuts between searching close-ups of Ricci, Bruno, and Baicco and the seemingly endless path of bikes and bike parts, a path which leads nowhere. Even camera movement reveals nothing, and as these tracking shots begin to fill with men on the street even these men appear to become like the objects they are selling, almost in the same outfits, with the same gestures, with the same faces.

Toward the end of the sequence, a threatening sexual tension unexpectedly occurs when Ricci and his friends leave Bruno—another physical break in the wandering bond of the father and son—to inspect a bicycle frame that looks suspiciously like the lost Fides. As they leave Bruno in this crowded hubbub of barking sellers, a tall man appears in the middle ground behind Bruno, blowing bubbles into the air, an image of meaningless effervescence floating in this sea of marketplace chattel. In a cut, Ricci's band of men confront a vendor in heated exchange about a bike frame he is painting, eventually calling a policeman to insist on seeing the serial number of the frame, which of course is not the stolen bike, and which of course begins to suggest the impossibility of finding the lost bike in this illusory quest, the indiscernible and unbridgeable line between the real and the imaginary. Meanwhile, Bruno looks casually through the bike parts piled in a stall until that tall stranger, presumably a child predator, approaches him. An insouciant and dapperly dressed man with stylish hat (distinguishing him from the busy and drab workers surrounding him), he leans over Bruno, hovering close to him as the boy attempts to turn away. "Would you like this bell," he asks, as he presses closer to the boy who uncomfortably looks away and shakes his head no. "Shall I buy one for you?" he continues. A peculiar moment in the midst of this hunt for a bicycle, the shot then cuts back to Ricci who returns with a policeman to inspect the suspect bike frame. Disappointed that the frame is not his stolen bike and baited by the vendor's ironically defiant shout that "we're all honest here in Piazza Vittoria," Ricci suddenly realizes—in a conjunction that crystallizes the lack of a pedestrian direction and the loss of familial orientation—"There's nothing more for us here," and he quickly asks, "Where is my son?" Finding him with the suspicious man, Ricci looks knowingly and viciously at him, as he pulls Bruno away.

Between the predator and the police, the social order has become strangely tense and stretched across fear and disorder, the interior disorientation between Ricci and Bruno matching the exterior disorientation of the Roman streets. More broadly, this moment reverberates, like another walk in the dark, backward and forward, through the broken image of a heteronormative family. Indeed, the fault lines of this fractured image had already opened the film when Ricci's wife and Bruno's mother had to pawn their wedding linens for a bicycle and that broken image completely shatters in the concluding images of the film when the father-son relationship begins to shatter before the crime of the father whose desperate and frantic theft of a bicycle converts him too into a bicycle thief. If earlier in the film Ricci and Bruno exchanged anxiously the bond of eyelines, in the end the two wandering pedestrians walk with stunned stares down a road into the distance, marching into the sunset among a faceless crowd with no clear destination. Have they become a version of Michel De Certeau's walking dead moving through a city in which they "elude legibility" even of each other? Walking through this city "the everyday has a certain strangeness" now, especially in this piazza where, as a truck driver remarks at the end of that sequence, "it rains everyday." What was once a mobility oriented by human agency, linearity, distinctions, and family is now "an opaque and blind mobility characteristic of the bustling city" (93). More exactly, a postwar city.

3

Describing . . . Vacancy: *Throne of Blood* (Akira Kurosawa, 1957)

The physical movements of the characters in Akira Kurosawa's *Throne of Blood* are, from my Western perspective, wildly demonstrative, almost ritualistically excessive, as if the difficult expression of their interior selves can barely be naturalized within the exterior world that surrounds them, as if the strenuous efforts to move speech and body requires continual deliberations within a space that threatens to absorb or to refuse them. I recognize of course the heritage of these characters in Japanese Noh theater, but something else seems to be happening in this astonishing adaptation of Shakespeare's

Describing Cinema. Timothy Corrigan, Oxford University Press. © Oxford University Press 2024.
DOI: 10.1093/oso/9780197625354.003.0004

Macbeth, something that short-circuits how the usual descriptions of characters moving in space can reveal meanings as the manifestation of intended and resulting actions. Which makes me wonder if Japanese *bunraku* puppet theater rather than Noh theater may be the more revealing source of this strain within description.

With this in mind, I connect my rubric "vacancy" to Roland Barthes's essay on bunraku, in which he notes that the Japanese puppeteers in these performances are fully visible on stage and so subvert the "motor link which proceeds from character to actor and which is always conceived, in the West as the expressive means of inwardness" (*Empire of Signs* 61). With bunraku, the secretive sources of Western theater "are exposed in their emptiness," and it abolishes the metaphysical link the West cannot help establishing between body and soul, cause and effect, motor and machine, agent and actor." In bunraku, Barthes continues, "the puppet has no strings. No more strings, hence no more metaphor, no more Fate; . . . man no longer a puppet in the divinity's hands, the *inside* no longer commands the *outside*" (62). In his essay for the Criterion DVD of *Throne of Blood,* Stephen Prince in turn relates this emptiness to the other East Asian tradition of ink paintings: "The striking emptiness of the spaces in the film—the skies, the dense rolling fog that obscures mountains and plains—is a cinematic rendition of *sumi-e* composition" (n.p.). As a variation on this idea of emptiness, I substitute the term "vacancy" as a way to emphasize the architectural structures and spaces that continually trouble human occupancy at the center of *Throne of Blood*—from the demon hut made of fragile sticks to the massive fortresses surrounded by open plains and hills.

With adaptations from a literary source to a film (such as this one), a similar notion of the vacancy might be applicable, particularly for this film. In this sense, this kind of adaptation becomes a variation on the typical models in adaptation studies where the interactions between two different textual discourses follow versions of a transactional exchange: adaptations as, for instance, intertextualities, as transpositions, as translations, where these transactions typically highlight gaps, shifts, and mergers of registers between, for instance, different historical periods, between literary sources and their cinematic adaptations, between literary authors and filmic auteurs, between high culture and popular culture, and so forth. With *Throne of Blood*, the adaptive transaction happens as a four-part movement—between eleventh-century Scotland, sixteenth-century Japan, Shakespeare's seventeenth-century England, and Kurosawa's post–World War II Japan—while the Shakespearean play and the postwar adaptation work as another transaction between the literary language of theater and the cinematic language of film. In the majority of adaptations, these transactions usually map a *productive* exchange implicitly and most commonly as a concrete measure of what motivates specific aesthetic gains and losses in the transactions (what is added to the adapting film and what is left out in the transaction, for instance). With *Throne of Blood*, however, this typical model of transactional exchanges overlooks, I believe, how the heart of this adaptation might be better described as an erasure of transactional value, as a vacating of the tragic action of *Macbeth* and its cathartic humanism, leaving only a timeless and placeless violence, the violence whose emptiness supersedes any human motivation, natural logistics, or productive exchange. What does it mean then if the focus of the adaptation is not tragic action but human and spatial vacancy?

Shakespeare's *Macbeth* identifies the threat of that vacancy at many points in its plot in which human life might become only sound and fury signifying nothing. But, in many interpretations, that pull toward a senseless nothing is overcome through the climactic action of Macbeth who turns to combat his foe MacDuff and thus to claim his fate and the tragic individuality in his death, concluding an almost Aristotelean movement of rise and fall. In the film *Throne of Blood*, however, a slew of arrows, mostly without onscreen sources, skewers and shreds that death and identity, enclosing Washizu in a space that constricts the human body more and more with each arrow, leaving his hysterically frantic eyes and flayed body searching for a human eyeline match to account for his end, which is more of a slaughter than a heroically tragic stand. If *Macbeth* is about fate, time, choice, and action, *Throne of Blood* is about architectural fragility and the violence of emptiness.

An earlier sequence forecasts and maps the vacancy that will be Washizu's death. After a forest demon foretells that he, Washizu, will become the most powerful leader of the land, the Lord of Spider's Web Castle, he and his wife Asaji plan the murder of the current leader, Lord Tsuzuki, when he intends to visit their fortress. As Tsukzuki and his entourage arrive later, Washizu runs back and forth through the empty "washitsu" room (could the spatial openness of this traditional tatami room be a source for Washizu's name?) in which Asaji sits motionless on the floor, the translucent shoji doors open so that the inside blends into the outside courtyard, her stillness contrasting sharply with the frenetic movement of horses and soldiers outside in the yard. When a nervous soldier screeches the unexpected arrival of the Lord and his forces ("thick with armed men from Spider's Castle"), Washizu races toward the open screens and then nervously returns to the room, turning around with jerky movements and a glaring expression, while Asaji kneels motionless in the background. Running directly toward the camera, he runs outside to gather his men to receive Tsuzuki and his entourage, staring fiercely into the distance in a medium close-up. A reverse shot then shows the arrival of the Lord's hunting party, accompanied by melodious, non-diegetic flute music.

Three key contrasts create a dynamic in this sequence that permeates the entire film: one between the still bent body of Asaji and the frenetic darting movements of Washizu, another between a sparsely expressive dialogue and the seemingly difficulty of the human voice to articulate its surroundings, and a third along the hazy line that separates the energy of an exterior space and the tightly controlled order of the minimalist interior. In the end each of these contrasts will collapse into the overwhelming other of inanimate bodies, inarticulate silence, and inhuman exteriors.

After two interim sequences in which Lord Tsuzuki reveals his plan to promote Washizu and Miki to new positions of power, the murder sequence unwinds through a series of architectural and spatial configurations. First, because Tsuzuki will stay in the master chamber for the night, two men prepare a nearby chamber for Washizu, a room where the former Lord, the "scheming traitor" Fujimaki, had committed suicide, a room in which "no scrubbing will clean the blood-stained floors," a room whose walls are so stained by treachery and violence (forming abstract undulations) that it has become barely inhabitable. Now in the room of human treachery and violence, Washizu walks, head bowed in thought, around a sleeping mat, while Asaji's voice-off urges him forward toward the murder ("Open your eyes and look for yourself. . . . If you let this night pass, such an opportunity will never come again"). Visually, she is tangentially there but only as a marginal force bent on tearing down the barriers of social and ethical restraint. Provoked, Washizu then moves rapidly across the room, again a movement on the run from something, looking left and right, and then at her as she sits immobile on the floor. Eyes turned away from him and his from her, she describes the plot to drug the guards, kill them, and accuse them of the murder. She rises and looks off in response to a bird's cry, which like all the questionable signs and sounds in the film, she interprets (wrongly) as harbinger of success. "Will you risk the world?" for this success, she asks Washizu, and under the repeated sounds of a shrill flute and percussive beats, she insists, "Ambition makes the man. . . . The cry is from heaven." The sounds of nature and the world are, however, in fact arbitrary and senseless. The couple couches before the lit torches of the passing servants, ghost-like behind the shoji screens. These rooms now seem haunted by a vacancy, even when human figures inhabit them, and the sounds of birds and musical instruments may or may not be part of the diegesis of the human world. Even when there may be a physical source for the sound, its force and significance beckon from far beyond that source and human society.

As Asaji glides across the room—propelled almost invisibly, like a nonhuman spirit without legs, before she kneels in front of the rigid figure of Washizu—the squeaking rustle of her kimono slides eerily through the silence. In a medium shot that fills the screen she suddenly disappears, almost sinks, into a dark void of a doorway. From the blackened interior of that doorway, as if from a black hole that absorbs and releases all the energy that comes near it, she then slowly remerges, statuesque, face and eyes staring nowhere, vacant, carrying the sleeping potion with which to drug the guards. Through the whistling rhythm of that flute, there is a cut: Asaji approaches the drugged and slumping guards and returns to the chamber with a spear, as the couple silently approach and stare into each other's eyes. Washizu snatches it with fierce inevitability, as if human will has finally been vanquished. A cut out to a slivered moon appears, and, again, the screech of the unseen preternatural bird rattles the silence. The outside of the natural/supernatural has entered this fragile inside. A close-up of Washizu's face violently grimaces, nearly shattering the surface of his rigid expression, a facial surface nearly out of control, on the verge of shattering: that face as mask inherited from Japanese theater turning inside out as a ferocious transformation in which the cold winds blowing outside could whisk away human expression, a dramatic and violent wiping away like the numerous edits of imagistic wipes in the film that slice through human action, logic, and continuity.

Unseen, unheard, in the still vacancy of night, the murder is done.

Asaji kneels slowly, eyes offscreen, head turning cautiously before she rises quickly to percussive beats and rapid flute notes. She begins a giddy *danse macabre* before a wall of arrows, one of so many walls that entice and buckle before the violence inside out. She stares at the blood stain on the floor, turning quickly to see Washizu marching from the right edge of the frame with the bloodied spear. With the act, space is now an otherworldly theater on a human stage, centered on almost paralyzed actors suffused with blood. From this moment on, the narrative, space, and bodies begin to come undone, dissolving into the surrounding space. The human world becomes the surface of a translucent shell—or a translucent hell.

I have always admired Thomas De Quincey's 1823 essay "On Knocking at the Gate in *Macbeth*," in which the loud banging on the castle gate the morning after the murder of Duncan breaks a profound silence that has protectively enclosed the castle space like a tomb, reflecting "back upon the murderer a peculiar awfulness and a depth of solemnity" (389). In *Throne of Blood*, as Asaji races to the gate screaming "Intruders!," hoping to cover up their crime, that profound silence and solemnity of Shakespeare's play have no place. Instead, the murder releases an explosion of chaotic noises and actions: shouts of betrayal, charging horses, and faceless soldiers knocking and tearing apart the banners and flags that offered a temporary and fragile sense of place and identity for the ruled and the rulers. Here, the paradox of vacancy, in the space where *Macbeth* becomes *Throne of Blood*, is that vacancy is neither still nor silent.

4

Describing . . . Ghosts: *Pyaasa* (Guru Dutt, 1957)

Describing a film or a sequence in a film can be sustained and galvanized by a vast range of experiences, including what one has read (about a specific film, film theory, or anything else!) or conversations with friends that surface, sometimes unconsciously, as part of a response to and description of a film. What happens then when a viewer, such as myself, has very little background or knowledge to fully grasp or to properly describe certain movies, limited by personal blind spots across different histories or different cultures. Which means there will inevitably be gaps, absences, and

Describing Cinema. Timothy Corrigan, Oxford University Press. © Oxford University Press 2024.
DOI: 10.1093/oso/9780197625354.003.0005

mistakes in an encounter with any film, as I experience with the Guru Dutts's 1957 *Pyaasa*, a movie canonized as a prominent part of the hierarchy of the auteurs of world cinema history, elevated as one of the ever-present specters within the history of global cinema, and, so in various degrees, seen but not fully seen by me and many others today. For any viewer with limited familiarity with a film, that film can seem sometimes to provide only traces of itself and to resist confident designations and explanations in explaining them. In this sense, my challenge in describing *Pyaasa* may be a common challenge for viewers of any film with which the partial knowledge of a descriptive spectator might foreground or exaggerate that "guessing game" that is part of any description. A limitation and challenge, I would add, that might also be a freedom. For such a viewer, that film might appear as a phantom of its historical and cultural realities, like a cinematic ghost, like an unexpected elevator meeting with a lost and barely recognized acquaintance after many years' absence.

Played by filmmaker Dutt, the autobiographical character Vijay is an idealistic ghost, a phantom poet who righteously chooses to expose the injustices of the material society around him (so profoundly different from the threatening phantoms of *Meet Me in St. Louis*). His trials and tribulations are both romantic and literary, leading to painful losses and misunderstandings at the intersection of both those worlds, eventually driving him to a kind of suicide as he willfully disappears from the world. In the melodramatic triangle of the plot, a destitute and impoverished Vijay gives a beggar his coat, and when that man is later killed by a train and subsequently mistaken for the poet, Vijay becomes a material ghost, dead but not dead. Meanwhile Gulabo, a young prostitute, discovers Vijay's discarded poems and falls in love with him through the image projected by those poems, eventually leading to his universal, ironically posthumous, fame.

Throughout, Vijay cannot escape the memories of his lost love Meena, his passionate partner from his youth but who is now married to the wealthy publisher Mr. Ghosh, Vijay's romantic and literary rival who is the main character and the emblem of the material brutality of this society that will ghost Vijay. How unintentionally appropriate that the surname of this embodiment of hostility recalls a contemporary idiom for willfully ignoring or making socially invisible a person or truth, since Vijay and his poetry, for much of the film, are quite literally "ghosted" by friends, family, lovers, and society. In the culminating irony of the film, Vijay, who has been declared dead but who is physically alive, is mistakenly perceived to be that dead beggar found in a railyard, rather than the presumed suicidal Vijay. When his friend (and comic relief) Abdul recognizes the actual Vijay in a hospital prison for the mentally disabled, Abdul can only confirm the spectatorial reality that troubles the entire film and my experience of it when he exclaims, "A ghost. Lord, please make it vanish."

But, unlike actual ghosts, material ghosts do not vanish. During a massive posthumous event honoring his now resurrected and popular poetry, the ghosted Vijay climactically appears in the doorway suffused with washed-out light at the back of a grand theater, the lighting alone making the physical reality of Vijay ambiguous. As the audience turns to see him emerging from the luminous light of the doorway, the image tracks back so that he steps forward as if from a cave of light, almost as if from a movie projector. The shock and incomprehension of the crowd at his appearance angrily turns to viciously ghost the resurrected ghost, an event that shifts the horror of this presumed haunting by a supernatural specter to the blindness of a social mob, in a whirlwind of chaotic darkness that seem to shroud the crowded auditorium, a surging crowd provoked of course by the financial greed of Ghosh. When Meena later confronts Vijay in the back rooms of the hall, he appears again like an apparition in the sunlit doorway, accepting his permanent place in the other world of film, in fact this film: "I'm going far away . . . to where I won't need to go farther," he quietly says. The couple then walks into the misty back of the frame, disappearing into the mystical somewhere else of celluloid. The broader irony here is that Vijay has been a specter from the beginning of the film, as the filmic embodiment of Guru Dutt, the other Vijay, the actor who embodies of the illusory character Vijay and the auteurist director of the film, who will himself, become seven years later, in the pressurized wake of the blockbuster success of *Pyaasa*, a real suicide victim (or so it is often presumed), a celebrated real ghost and, in a sense, a victim of his own film.

Ghosts inhabit the past, even as they haunt the present, wandering that gap between past and present through flashbacks throughout the film, between the lost memories of Meena and the socially unseeable future with the prostitute Gulabu. This gaping space opens dramatically almost midway through the film when Vijay re-encounters Meena, years after their derailed romance, in an elevator just after he has been hired by her husband Ghosh and years after she has abandoned him and their young love for Ghosh's material wealth and comfort. As the elevator door opens, Vijay appears about to enter a medium close-up, the upper part of his face blackened by a shadow while his mouth and chin are brightly illuminated, with the background wall lit with a parallel contrastive graphic of split spaces of light and dark, part of the many binary oppositions and contrasts used throughout the design of the film. As he moves forward into the light, the image tracks back and then cuts and zooms forward to Meena inside the elevator whose piercing eyes rise in surprised recognition. As often in the film, zooms and tracks become the visual shapes of character's desires and yearnings whose rapidly dramatic movements also suggest their evanescence. A counter shot captures the weak smile of Vijay in close-up as he greets her with equally piercing eyes, eyes that beckon but hide an invisible emotional reality that cannot now ever be realized—notably with words—by the former lovers. A shot/ counter shot exchange of intense eyeline matches continues to expand the tight elevator space between them into a vibrant other world that is then counterpointed by the arrival onto the elevator of a small group of people that crowd the couple into a corner. Even in an elevator, there is the strain that occurs throughout the narrative between the unseen face of private romance and the faceless anonymity of public insensitivity and intrusion.

The camera moves across the back of Vijay's head as he turns toward the blurred, unfocused, and vaguely smiling face of Meena, a shimmering and fading reflection, a face lit to almost seem a deathmask image, as a flashback transitions the scene to their vanished past, a scene that surfaces as Vijay and Meena stroll past a party with waltzing couples. In a medium shot, they sit, while they glance back at the harmonious society of dancers that they will never be part of. Unaware of their invisibility, Meena then gazes rapturously up at him. In a narrative already populated by lost people and lost lovers, this first flashback reveals another, even more distant world, a fantasized world beyond the grave of their present reality, now signaled by Vijay's strained, almost confused, look into a past vanishing before his eyes, followed by a cut to a painfully worried close-up of Meena, eyes down. They sit in the dark of an existence that, even as a cinematic flashback, seems long lost across Vijay's distanced look and within Meena's buried eyes. She almost speaks; he almost speaks. But that would be impossible in this silent grave of the past.

As the fading image tracks in on Vijay's barely visible face, the strummed string music marks another transition, now a doubled flashback into a deeper past, a deeper grave, beyond the real present time, and even beyond the first romantic layer of the flashback, into a cloud and smoke-filled realm that, as one commentator once put it, could only exist on an elaborate soundstage—or, in this film, beyond the material world that has crushed and exiled Vijay and into the false promise of cinematic redemption. With stylized props of moons and planets hanging above the stage (balloons with strings whose artificiality and theatricality forsakes much of the social realism of the film in order to find a filmic resurrection), the dark figure of Meena dances down an open staircase from nowhere into the clouds below, descending quickly as the image cuts to the blackened outline of Vijay who enters in a cut through a baroque gateway and fence, under a Victorian street lamp, surrounded by billowing clouds. Dark contrastive highlighting and shimmering unfocused images suggest a world on the verge of disappearing, where the dramatic tracks describe a never-to-be settled world of longing for another world.

A shot/counter shot edit of their close-ups begins their duet about love and desire, "Hum Aap Ki Aankhon Mein," a teasing musical dialogue about dreams, eyes, and punishments, while they sway rhythmically, in counter-shot medium close-ups, through the clouds at their feet and the sheer drapery separating them like clouds. They sway through a series of alternating musical questions and responses:

> What if I settle this heart in your eyes?
> What if I shut my eyes and punish your heart?
> What if I steal the sleep from your eyes?
> I shall fall at your feet in utter distress.
> What if I don't even fan my veil to comfort you?
> What if I shut my eyes and punish your heart?

As the clouds rise beneath their feet and in one long shot, cutting off the lower parts of their bodies, this is a utopian encounter in the heavens, the spinning couple harmonized physically, emotionally, and musically, as never before and as never will be. The baroque iron work in the foreground and the string of receding lamp lights create an ominous vanishing point in the background as a reminder of their own vanishing, as they dance off screen leaving an empty space behind the sheer and shearing curtains that obstruct the foreground.

They continue to address each other through song, seductively and teasingly. In an overhead long shot they then part and disappear into corners of the image. Now alone, Vijay moves perplexed and saddened through the enclosing draperies, looking off screen toward the vanished Meena who, in a cut, is seen dancing back up the staircase toward the large artificial moon at the top. Harp chords lead Vijay back to the bench of the first layer of the flashback where he looks down at the place next to him where the ghost of Meena previously sat. Walking to the front of the image, he retrieves a piece of paper, and a cut returns him to the present time, the elevator, and the close-up of Meena. What is the message on this scrap of paper from beyond that absorbs him? His poems? Meena's note of love? Through her longing glances, she asks, "How have you been," and he replies, with stunning irony, "I'm alive." As the elevator doors open, she says, "I forgot I was going up." She follows him with poignant eyes, as the elevator door closes again. Barely alive, I would say, left below the ground that Meena rises above.

How could this film not remind me of Gliberto Perez's *The Material Ghost*, whose title serves as a metaphor for a broad cinematic aesthetic that links, in that study, so many modern filmmakers and auteurs? According to Perez, many films share a fundamental principle in creating moving specters of the real, whose images create ghostly figures and worlds through which viewers enter other realms, real, not real, less than real, more than real. "The film image is the true hallucination, the material ghost," Perez writes. "The images on the screen carry in them something of the world itself, something material, and yet something transposed, transformed into another world" (28). In *Pyaasa*, describing the ghosts of this other world is made especially complicated because that ghost is both a character—the actor Guru Dutt as Vijay—and the filmmaker Guru Dutt. If a corrupt publishing industry and materialistic lover transform Vijay into a specter barely visible to the society around him, the film has materialized the auteur Dutt as a haunted and haunting image, ironically destined to possibly fulfill the fate of Vijay, his afterlife materialized by the cinematic ghost in the film and by the ghost that is the film.

5

Describing . . . Exposure: *Contempt* (Jean-Luc Godard, 1963)

In Jean-Luc Godard's *Contempt,* contempt is a house under con-
struction, a transparent maze built with obtrusive walls, furniture, clothing, and languages, where relationships collapse
and movies are made. It is a bristling atmosphere as searing as a
Mediterranean sun in summer, brightly illuminating a world of primary colors, as precarious as a building perched on a cliff above
a vast sea, tottering like a troubled marriage. Beginning with the
opening credit sequence in which Raoul Coutard's camera tracks
forward to the front of the frame and then turns on us, the film
exposes and implicates even viewers like me and desires like ours
as complicitous—a word that lingers through much of the film—in
its contemptible architecture. Here and there, the relentless movement of the film opens multiple exposures, of a place with too many
conflicting frameworks, of emotions that fade in the harsh light of
language, of the films to desire.

Describing Cinema. Timothy Corrigan, Oxford University Press. © Oxford University Press 2024.
DOI: 10.1093/oso/9780197625354.003.0006

Contempt explores two salient houses linked by an open doorway, both houses built of language, sex, and money. First, there is the house of turmoil that entwines Paul Javal's job to script a film with his attempted (re)construction of his marriage to Camile Javal, played by Bridget Bardot, an impossible rehabilitation of too many walls and too many deceptions. Second is the expansive house of language that offers the tools for the communicative possibility or impossibility for that reconstruction. In this second house, the stuttering adaptation of a work of classic literature, Homer's *Odyssey*, produced through tongue-tied conversations between an auteur, an iconic German director Fritz Lang, and a crass American producer, Jeremy Prokosch, becomes the fractured linguistic blueprint for the tragically comic role of language throughout the film, mockingly summarized in a translator's continual mistranslations in the first part of the film. In the perpetually unstable and unfinished gaps in these houses, contempt seethes and roils through an impossible movie, through an unfinished home, and through almost nonsensical conversations in this desperately talky film. Here nothing fuels contempt more than the loves and hates lingering within their incomplete lives and before their unfinished doorways and misspoken sentences.

Here is how Leo Bersani and Ulysses Dutoit pose a key question: "What does contempt do to cinematic space? How does it affect the visual field with which Godard works, and especially the range and kinds of movement allowed for in that space?" (21-22). Beginning in the Cincettà studios and ending in the magnificent Casa Malaparte on the Isle of Capri, the answer to that question occurs most incisively midway through the film, in Paul and Camille's unfinished apartment. After an opening shot of the exterior balconies of a modern apartment building, Paul's job, their relationship, and the apartment immediately interlock inside: Camille asks how much Paul is being paid for the script he is writing. Enough money, he replies, that "we can finish off paying for the apartment." As they move in and out of the entryway and the three different rooms connected to it, their conversation is domestically banal. Meanwhile Paul removes his tie, the beginning of a cycle of dressing and undressing in a way that parallels the constant making and unmaking of this home and their conversation. As they mildly bicker about who will be first in the bath, Paul exits by opening a door with a missing center panel which he then reenters through the same open panel without opening the door. Unhung doors lean against the wall, and a paint can sits in the background on the floor. Throughout the sequence, doors that usually offer privacy and connections instead suggest a foundational and fluid deterioration of the balances between the spaces in this relationship. Without demarcations, there is only desperate movement and conflict, and with so much movement, there is no home.

The center of this apartment as house is, appropriately, that entryway, a transitional place which in fact acts more as an exit way, through which the movement of the characters repeatedly exposes the empty frames of this never completed home and relationship. As the two shuffle constantly between the rooms, Paul reads a letter on a bright red sofa next to a bright blue chair, part of the Technicolor primaries that permeate the film to create a kind of comic book theatricality within which Paul and Camille struggle to act. She tosses a book on a coffee table and moves off, into a medium shot from the foyer that reframes her through one doorway on the right and him through another doorway on the left, where a classic statue of a woman, perhaps Greek, stands against the wall in the foreground, at one point vertically paralleling the figure of Camille, a Penelope without a home. "I bought something today," Camille says, while Paul crosses behind the wall in the foreground into the framed hallway where she was just previously standing and where he continues to undress, asking, "What thing?" He enters part way into the bedroom where Camille hides behind the door wearing her new black wig, the first of several signs that she is no longer she for him or just another she in the moving cycle of sex for men. Normal clothing and theatrical costumes are indistinguishable, and both are constantly coming on and off in a prosaically and repetitiously desperate and disparate drama of finding some self and some stability.

Within this rolling tension, Paul's earlier flirtation with a female script assistant and his apparent sexual dangling of Camille before the lecherous Prokosch become concentrated on their impending visit to the Capri villa. "Do you want to go to Capri?" Paul calls from outside the room, a question fraught with an implicit or impending sexual betrayal of Camille that rattles the space of the apartment and the house of language itself. Unhung pictures and books on the floor lean against the wall, and "I won't say no and I won't say yes either" is Camille's delayed and incomplete answer to his question. Which is, of course, no answer but another suspended and exposed undoing of the idea of a communicative dialogue.

A cut follows her from the entryway as she crosses the hallway to the living room, with Paul's bare legs appearing in the background as he sits half-dressed on the toilet. "He invited you," he calls. Truncated and fractured bodies drift across the mise-en-scène. As she navigates through the bright red furniture, arranging the pins for her new dark wig, and backed by the plaintiff and unpredictable string chords of the musical motif, she shouts, "Where did we put the mirror?" and glances—as a moment of recognition, I think—at the metal and hollow female statue who may be her true mirror image. Paul calls from the bathroom, "Not at all; we're both invited," as she walks from the entryway into the adjoining hallway. "Look," she says about her new look, walking into the bathroom where Paul sits in the bathtub with a hat on and cigar in mouth. "I prefer you as a blonde," he says, and she counters, "I prefer you without a hat and cigar." Like the movie actors that they are and that they play, they have become things, objects, costumes, props, living the horror and abyss of the nonchalance that permeates their lives and their conversations. If according to Heidegger "language is the house of being," this is a house of nonbeing, of linguistic innuendo and confrontation built on an unspeakable void of sexual betrayal.

The stalled progress of the apartment renovations and the slow deterioration of the marriage now become reflected in a series of temporal miscommunications and maladaptations, oblique and paradoxical linguistic movements, moving forward and backward as an exposure of temporal relativity and disorder. This is no doubt a version of the miscommunications and maladaptations that pressures Lang's film adaptation of *The Odyssey* and, with reflexive irony, Godard's own adaptations of Alberto Moravia's novel *A Ghost at Noon* as this film. As Camille combs her hair, *Contempt* shifts into an oblique allegory about the stuttering relationship between language and cinema, an allegory in which Paul inhabits the cinematic and Camille the linguistic, two mutually incomprehensible discourses, parodied by the script girl's constant mistranslations of French, Italian, German, and English throughout the film. "I just look like Dean Martin in *Some Came Running*," he says, doubling the connection among the movies, these centerless characters, and his changing sense of self. Across a conversation that moves in and out of the central room, she counters the Dean Martin reference with a damning verbal pun based on a children's folktale that plays on the word "*l'âne*" for donkey (and in English for "ass"): "You want to look like Dean Martin, but it's more like Martin's ass." She then describes the tale as she leaves the room, "One day he goes to Bagdad to buy a flying carpet. He finds this really pretty one. He sits on it but it doesn't fly. The merchant replies 'Not surprising. If you want to fly you mustn't think of an ass. Ok, I won't think of one. But automatically he thinks of one, so the carpet doesn't fly." Reentering the main room of the apartment, wrapped in a sheet, resembling the toga of a Roman senator as a new persona, Paul answers with a response that summarizes the widening break of miscommunication: "I don't get. What does it have to do with me?" and Camille explains by refusing to explain: "Exactly what I was saying." A moral of this communication allegory. Thought is exposure, and Paul is incapable of it.

Within marriage, filmmaking, and financial transactions, these versions of maladaptation as miscommunication create the prominent layers of *Contempt*. In an important sense, the languages of communication—as images and as language—become the deteriorating mortar of this house, and, like the house itself, mark all understandings and misunderstandings with the thinly disguised or avoided ripples of deconstructive contempt. Paul's contempt for Camille, and her for his arrogance and stupidity. Within this house of combative discourses, contempt becomes a kind of refusal to see and to speak: When Paul asks: "Why do you have contempt for me?" Camille answers, "That, I'll never tell you, even if I were dying." Then there is the silence, a muted void exposed within language and within the film.

As Camille clears the dishes from the table, the room becomes a kind of echo chamber of denial and evasion, leaving "nothing" as a verbal space for "the obvious." He sits on a room partition, still smoking his cigar, and attempts a rapprochement: "You've been acting weird today. What's wrong?" he interjects. As she exits, foreclosing even the question: "Nothing at all. . . . I knew you'd say that. It's nothing I simply I said you're an ass." Paul walks in circles while she speaks from another room, and then he knocks on the two breasts and then the stomach of the metal statue, creating a metallic echo of emptiness as a metaphoric nothing or at least confusion. "Not the same sound all over," he remarks. "Why don't you want to go to Capri?" As she returns to the room, offering more non-sequitur responses: "Because you're an ass." He suddenly slaps her face, followed by a close-up of the back of her head that then turns to a profile: "You frighten me, Paul. It's not the first time." She, then he, apologizes, and a medium close-up cuts to their lower bodies, she in a red towel and he in a white toga, that shows her leg lift between his leg, then releasing herself in a medium shot. The vestiges of sexual desire that immediately wilt.

Those two thematic registers now crisscross more conspicuously than ever, exposing both in the process: that of the troubled marital relationship, and that of their home finances inseparable from the movie business. While Paul leaves through a coffee-table book of erotic frescoes, static images of desire that have no place or every place in this home without equilibrium or rest, she prepares a sofa as a bed, and they continue to bicker, his continual (but ingenuous) confusion about what he did wrong and she refusing to answer him. Convinced that he has changed because of the "movie people," she reminiscences about when he happily wrote crime novels, despite not making much money. Saying he no longer wishes to go to Capri, he picks up the photo book, and sitting on the couch, he looks through a series of pictures, close-ups of erotic frescos and statues in different fornicating positions. They talk across the distance of different rooms, through walls and non sequiturs: he reads about judging the beauty of three nude women and then suggests, "we'll just mortgage the flat when we run out of money," and she responds inadvertently making the central connection, "Something makes you think I've stopped loving you?" He enters the bathroom where she reads out loud from a book on Fritz Lang, in the bathtub, about negative and positive worldviews, Greek tragedy, rebellion against conventions, and even whether to kill an unfaithful partner because "killing is never a solution." Language again becomes a wrecking ball. When he scolds her use of a "vulgar" word ("con"/jerk), saying "it doesn't suit" her, she offers a litany of such words in close-up, such "asshole" and "son of a bitch." "Do you still think it doesn't suit me?" she says as she leaves the bathroom. Language degenerates as space contracts without the promise, or even the hint, of a narrative solution.

Nostalgia briefly replaces lucidity. Recalling their past life of romantic "complicity," they recount that narrative in a montage of past and future events, but that constructed montage seems a mechanical attempt to wallpaper over the exposed emptiness of this house, to fill it with images from the past that can be narrated only as disconnected fragments. As Paul finishes putting on his pants and shoes, he follows her through the apartment, with the hollow metal statue at one point becoming part of the triangular arrangement of three fated figures. The subsequent montage of awkwardly posed inserts shows her when "we used to live in delicious complicity. . . and enchanted recklessness": bland, parodic flashback images of her in nature, reading in her black wig, spread naked on her stomach on a bright blue rug, talking to her mother on the bed, her naked on a red blanket. Over a flash forward to the deck of the Capri house, he notes, "She wasn't unfaithful, or she only seemed to be . . . the truth remained to be proven, despite appearances," followed by another flash forward to Camille about to join Prokosch in his red sports car, "I noticed that the more we doubt, the more we cling to false lucidity." Cut to another naked shot of her on a white rug, "in the hope of rationalizing what feelings have made murky."

They return to the present, walking their separate ways through the demarcated interior spaces. With the musical chords rising, Paul moves again through the open panel of a door, simultaneously opening the door for no reason, and sitting down to continue to type his scenario. Gestures without meaning. Now in a different dress, as a different person, Camille enters through the open panel and proclaims, ambiguously, about a murky past that no longer exists, "I love you exactly as before." She wanders into the hallway with a room in the background, cluttered with a ladder and cans and painting materials, that she then enters, offering the impossible possibility of leaving the glare of these rooms as the exposed center of all that they do, "What would you do if I stopped loving you?" "I wouldn't do the script and we'd sell the apartment." "This is idiotic . . . I love you," she says and then agrees to go to Capri, explaining, with chilling clarity, why: "I want to keep the apartment." She leaves the room, while Paul continues to type, the audial volume increasing. The camera tracks forward to show a picture of a grand (wedding?) spectacle in a massive theater, holding for several seconds on an image that is only an image without a reality in this house. As she flips through that art book of nudes, more images unadaptable to this life, she speaks on the phone to Prokosch about the movie and their coming to Capri. The movie, the apartment, and the relationship have, in advance, vanished into the burning sun.

In the final scene of the sequence, Camille accidentally drops and breaks some plates in the kitchen, more sounds that echo through an atmosphere tangibly strained by the vividly visual vicissitudes of contempt. Camille moves through the rooms and retrieves a page of the script from Paul's desk. She bitterly dismantles another façade, another empty inside: "Why not look for ideas in your head instead of stealing them." As they move round the apartment, tugging at each other, arguing about whether to go to Capri, Paul announces the end of the relationship in the service of the movie and the apartment: "Since I said yes to Prokosch, so long tenderness!"

In a medium shot, they sit in the blue chairs across from each with a white table lamp in between them. The medium close-up tracks between the two, interrupted and punctuated by the lamp light flicking on and off between them; he wearing his hat and smoking, and she in her black wig. Notably this is anything but the conventional shot/counter exchange that spatially bonds two alternating close-ups together; rather, it is a slow track that emphasizes the distance and obstructions between the two. Off screen, while the moving shot focuses on the lamp shade, the precise emblem of exposure in film where too much light is too much truth, he comments with painfully slow emphasis on each word the relentless dissolution of their relationship in this blinking light without enlightenment, "You said you loved me, and I should accept it. I'm sure you lied." "What's the use of knowing the truth?" she replies. "It's true I don't love you anymore. . . . Now it's over." As he prods her with questions she waffles, and suddenly a physical fight erupts in the middle of the room, with slaps and pushes. She dons a black sweater, musical chords rising again, and leaves the apartment, calling, "I despise you." Departing for the Capri house, they arrive at a villa that is primarily open decks and surrounding sea, an inverted corollary of their deconstructed apartment, a space fully exposed to the outside world of the Mediterranean, where, seen finally in a horizontal track, there is nothing on the panned horizon of this future.

The opening epigraph in *Contempt* misassigns—or maybe intentionally maladapts—a quotation from Michel Mourlet ascribed here to André Bazin: "The cinema substitutes for our gaze a world that corresponds to our desires." In a film about the desires for marriage, the desires for communication, the desires for money and material, the desires for a home, and the desires for cinema, Mourlet/Bazin's classical gaze and its traditional correspondences ironically crumbled in houses with too many barriers, too many unfinished cluttered spaces, too many broken mistranslations, too much exposure, releasing only frustration and contempt for the ruse of their promises. Instead, desire finds not a corresponding reality but only obstructions, fleeing movements, and silent lies. At one point in the film, Lang famously notes that the open spaces and wide angles of CinemaScope are only good for "showing snakes and funerals"—which are of course the chief figures and narrative events that describe *Contempt.*

6

Describing . . . Immobility: *The Conformist* (Bernardo Bertolucci, 1970)

About halfway through *The Conformist*, in 1938, Marcello Clerici meets his former university professor, Luca Quadri, in the office of Quadri's Paris home-in-exile. Their conversation turns to a classroom lecture and discussion from years ago about Plato's allegory of the cave in which the philosopher famously describes the human condition as analogous to prisoners chained in a cave with their backs to the entrance. A fire between the prisoners and the entrance casts shadows of the real figures outside the cave on the rear of the wall, shadows that the prisoners mistake for reality rather than for the shadows they are. The prisoners are immobile, and that state of

Describing Cinema. Timothy Corrigan, Oxford University Press. © Oxford University Press 2024.
DOI: 10.1093/oso/9780197625354.003.0007

immobility suffuses Bertolucci's entire film, set largely in Paris, where Italian fascist Clerici plots to assassinate the anti-fascist Quadri. Beyond the larger platonic argument about reality versus imagistic reflections of it, the immobility of those prisoners is what resonates throughout the film for me, as a binary paired with a repressed mobility. Indeed, these resonances of immobility turn on me as a viewer who, as Jean Louis Baudry ("Le dispositive") famously argued in 1975 about theatrical viewing in dark movie theaters, watches flickering images in my seat in the dark, as if in a waking dream. Can descriptive writing mobilize a viewer as a more mobile counter-current?

Here I need to argue a distinction: mobility and immobility are not here tantamount to motion and lack of motion. The former pairing usually assumes human agency; the latter often not: for me, mobility and immobility imply a driver, an agent, who can, who cannot, who chooses to make or not to make choices to propel a self or the vehicles for that self in one direction or another. Motion moves on its own or at least without human agency. I am mobile or immobile; clouds are in motion or not in motion. The implied difference might be metaphysical, existential, a bit over-refined, or, in 1938 Europe, profoundly political. *The Conformist* is then a movie about the agency of mobility and the paralysis of that agency as forms of immobility, the ferocious and destructive immobility of a fascist ideology that in this film is also a psychological repression. (Rewatching this film in the fall of 2022, I can't help but see those resonances ironically and sadly continue in the Italian election of ultra-conservative Giorgia Meloni as prime minister, where the renewal of that fascist history and campaign often claims to be, in large part, a response to a perceived threat: mobility as global migration and immigration.)

Immobility takes many shapes and spreads through the film, invariably contrasted with the possibility or refusal of the mobility it seeks to arrest: as a fascist political ideology entrenched in an imaginary past, often associated with the stable homogeneity of a mythologically pure race; as a social normalcy whose power excludes all disruptions of alternative races, religions, and underclasses; as a sexual rigidity that refuses desires and relationships other than heteronormative positions; as classical architectural spaces that structurally overcast, contain, and enclose the directions and movements of the characters; and, lastly, as the constrictive framing of image throughout the film that seems to extend and double each of those other immobilities in the sort of *mise-en-abyme* that description struggles to describe.

Specific figures of immobility extend through Clerici's past and present, including an institutionalized father who willingly binds himself into a straightjacket, and a mother who barely moves from her bed, imprisoned in her morphine cocoon. Isn't the plot of the film itself anchored in a classical logic of immobility, locked, it seems, in the determining presence of an early trauma from which any action and development cannot move beyond? Doesn't even Clerici's misrecognition of that childhood trauma—when he is sexually accosted and awakened by Lino, the chauffeur, whom he then shoots and thinks he has killed—become an immobile point that might or might not provide an explanation for Clerici's insistent need for the normalcy, for a bland marriage to Guilia ("paltry, little ambitions—all bed and kitchen"), for the need spoken to a blind friend of finding "Normalcy, Stability, Security," and for the almost quiet penultimate stoppage of *The Conformist* in a room with Clerici's own child and wife before a mural of a static blue sky where even the clouds lack motion? It all ends almost where it begins in 1938, halts there, only to be meanwhile spun back through the course of the film as a whirlwind of flashbacks. That classical narrative found in so many films to promise a forward movement is here placed in a fixated past, barely containing the rapid flashbacks that will lead back to 1938. A fixation that only becomes undone later in 1943 by that platonic prisoner, who will dare to move ever so slightly, to turn and look, perhaps to undo it all.

Contrasting this historical and formal immobility is the possibility of a disruptive mobility, which will begin to pressure Clerici in the second half of the film. In a transitional sequence, Giulia and Clerici's wife Anna, both elegantly dressed and now linked in a flirtatious emotional and sexual bond, run across a medium-long shot into a dance hall surrounded by large windows made up of multiple smaller glass frames, creating the box-like structure of a glass enclosure surrounding a crowd of dancing couples. As the two women rise hand in hand toward the dance floor, the blurred faces of Quadri and Clerici peer, like phantoms, suspiciously, statically, through separate exterior window frames in the background; the women and dancers separated from the imposing glances of the men in the window. The seated crowd of middle-class couples stare—fascinated? shocked?—at the two stunning women, and then a cut to the men who enter the building and sit in a booth, discussing a blank letter Quadri gave to Clerici. As a kind of trap, Quadri remarks, he had assumed Clerici would have used the letter to betray the anti-fascist resistance in Italy: "You would've used it against our friends in Rome.... I thought it best to put you through a test." At first this strikes me as a particularly peculiar moment: an odd bond between this pair of opposed men playing dangerous tricks with confidentiality, manipulation, and treachery; a bond that strangely links them in a stationary dance of death. Contrasting dramatically with the two women who rhythmically fold into each other on the dance floor, dipping smoothly to the accordion tango (a dance originally associated with male couples). Then a close-up of their upper bodies and faces shifting sensually with the music, erotically on the move. Mobility has become gendered.

Then the odd, perhaps explanatory, cut to a close-up of a Laurel and Hardy photograph, pasted on the exterior of the window of the dance hall, the same window against which Clerici sits inside the interior, making the photo appear as if stuck to the back of his motionless head. This is an image that might test, for most of us, the abilities (or excesses!) of interpretive description. Is the photo there for a laugh, as someone suggested? Or a reflexive cinematic gesture about comic film stars within this film about image-making, suggesting that this is a world of only images, like the world of those platonic prisoners? Possibly both, yet more, I think, as the emphatic short zoom into it might indicate: it is one of the several important and oppositional pairings in this sequence and in the entire film, which highlights a bond locking those bonded figures in a kind of defining embrace, that of the contrastive but mutually absorbed women, Giulia and Ana, that of Clerici and his fascist partner Manganiello (also seated in the dance hall), and, most prominently, that of the anti-fascist Quadri and the fascist Clerici. (As an extension of this constellations of pairings, in his monograph *Il Conformista*, Christopher Wagstaff makes another oblique connection for the Giulia and Anna pair, with Robert Aldrich's 1968 *The Killing of Sister George*, in which a lesbian couple, George and Childe, visit a lesbian bar dressed as Laurel and Hardy.)

But the photo is not merely a comic or reflexive re-inscription of those pairings. As I thought about it, this comic couple featuring a bully and an adult child from the 1920s and 1930s, the photo began to suggest a kind of an ironic master/slave paradigm in which their cartoonish and often violent gags never produced resolution or development or the possibility of moving on. Beckett's Vladimir and Estragon in fascist Italy. With his silly Hitler moustache, Hardy's well-known refrain, "Well, here's another mess you've gotten me into," could be uttered by Clerici or Manganiello. Or Laurel's well-known line from *Oliver the Eight* might become an ironic motto for much of Bertolucci's film: "I was dreaming I was awake, but I woke up and found meself [*sic*] asleep."

After lingering on the photo, a cut returns to the two women seductively dancing in fluid mobile circles, hand in hand, surrounded by an outer circle of intrigued onlookers, fascinated by the rotating pair. A frowning Clerici barks from the booth, "They must stop dancing," to which the bemused Quadri replies, "But why? They're both so beautiful." No doubt, I think, that this same-sex eroticism has rattled the strict framework of Clerici's heteronormative stability, an immobile normative unable to process the supposed violation of this open dance of other desires and emotions. A cut back to the kneeling Anna, looking intently at Guilia, holding her visually as she moves back and forth to the music, twirling in close-ups before they fall laughing into each other's arms. From the blur of their embrace, in a high-angle medium shot, Guilia circles the interior of the surrounding with unaccustomed independence and energy: "Well, what's there to stare at? This is Paris and I'm a fashionable woman, aren't I?" She grabs one member of the surrounding crowd and begins leading a long line of dancers, a farandole, in a twirling circle, spinning exuberantly around the room to the music, a blurred whirlwind.

The women then pull Quadri from the booth, and the long line of dancers now circles the room from outside the ubiquitous window frames, the circular movement graphically contrasting the plethora of rectangular frames that contain and freeze so much of the potential movement in the film. An overhead shot follows, capturing an isolated Clerici, in a far corner of the room, and the especially brutal Manganiello, a fascist henchman, among the very few who have refused the conga line. In a crosscut to medium shots of the two plotting assassins, Clerici and Manganiello, each taps their hand rhythmically to the music, their bodies unconsciously swept up in the insistent movement. In a long shot, Clerici then crosses the near empty dance floor and tells Manganiello that their target, Quadri, leaves in the morning, brusquely pushing this other Hardy away while insisting, incorrectly, that Anna, the lover whose mobility he cannot control, will not be with him to complicate the assassination. Despite his determination, however, she will again, independently, be on the move the next day.

As the line of dancers bounces back into the room in the foreground, the now diminutive figure of Manganiello sits alone in the background. Led by the two women across an extreme high-angle shot, the group creates a snaking circle around Clerici. As the coil of dancers tightens around the confused Clerici, sweeping him up in their movement, Manganiello leaves across the back of the room. In two overhead shots that capture the spinning top of dancers, the circling crowd grows and tightens more and more around Clerici whom they absorb into the inevitable momentum that will carry him and history forward. A cut to a concerned Manganiello, who watches through the window from outside, while a close-up depicts Quadri and a drunk and flirtatious Guilia dancing together and then gradually disappearing into the swaying bodies around them. Anna and Clerici now appear in the foreground where she tells him she'll be leaving with her husband on the ill-fated trip out of Paris. "You must remain," he quickly retorts with a desperate attempt to stop her flight preemptively before her life will be physically stopped.

A critically prominent undercurrent throughout the film, sexuality emerges here as a key mobility that threatens Clerici's relentless demand for normalcy, stability, and security. After a cut to Guilia flirting and kissing Quadri, Anna explains her departure to the desperately enamored and increasingly conflicted Clerici, noting that, despite appearances, Giulia "can't stand me." In a tight close-up while they dance, Clerici retorts that Giulia admires her, "she finds you seductive." Sexuality rising to the surface of the room, Guilia shouts over the dancers and music, "Anna! The professor is propositioning me!" This is followed by a cut to Anna and Clerici in a passionate embrace as they dance. In a slow reverse track, they disappear into the movement of the packed dance floor. The constant pull and push of the sexual desires of two women and two men about to be carried away on the rapid current of those desires within a political landscape that will not tolerate them. A virtual shock cut to an immobile Clerici sitting in the dark back seat of a car the next day, pursuing Quadri and Anna on an isolated snowy forest road.

In this mythical forest, Clerici and an anonymous band of fascists hunt down Quadri in a tragic adaptation of Stan Laurel's dreamlike forest outside Paris. While the faceless assassins stab to death Quadri, a classical Roman philosopher, a modern Julius Caesar struck down by a modern Brutus, Clerici sits stoically, unmoving, behind the window of his car. Pleading outside the window, Anna screams and begs him to save her before she flees the car window frame into the thick forest, where the killers chase her through the misty woods and viciously shoot her.

A flash forward to the resignation of Mussolini and his fascist dictatorship in 1943. Within the normalcy of his family, Clerici puts his daughter in a crib under a large wall mural with blue skies and white clouds, static clouds, without motion, waiting for mobility. He then leaves the house for the streets and wanders through throngs of anti-fascist celebrants and discovers Lino, the seducer from his youth whom he realizes he in fact had not killed years ago. Sitting on street steps behind the bars of a gate in a medium close-up, Clerici, the now-conscious prisoner in the cave of history moves, turns his head to look past the bars behind him, to know, to see for the first time, a truth too late.

7

Describing . . . Red: *Don't Look Now* (Nicolas Roeg, 1973)

Around 1995, I ran with my three young children through the dark labyrinthine streets of Venice, in retrospective a rather cruel paternal game about vague shadows seen around corners, hiding unseen dangers. Maybe I was replaying the parental angst of Nicholas Roeg's *Don't Look Now*, a film about the horrors of unseen anticipation that had haunted my vision of Venice for many years, an anticipatory angst that was also a memory of fleeing children and lost childhood. So there I was in Venice, the looker looked at through the lens of a movie, seeing flashes of red on the peripheries of every frame.

Color has purportedly served cinematic realism since the Technicolor realisms of the 1930s; but the color red has more often,

Describing Cinema. Timothy Corrigan, Oxford University Press. © Oxford University Press 2024.
DOI: 10.1093/oso/9780197625354.003.0008

I think, disturbed realism in the name of fantasies (and sometimes fearful fantasies), where even in classical movies like *Meet Me in St. Louis* it marks the nostalgic transformation of realism into fantasy. On that razor's edge between realisms and fantasies, I wonder, though: Why does the color red seem especially disturbing? I think of even mainstream films like Powell and Pressburger's *Red Shoes* (1948) or Steven Spielberg's *Schindler's List* (1993), where red overtakes or rattles the color scheme of the film and its stake in realism, placed on the margins of realism, creating a glimpse of another world of fears and hopes and passions. One of the early developers of the Technicolor process, Natalie Kalmus, wrote in 1935 that red elicits "a feeling of danger, a warning" and is able to "suggest the phases of life" from love and happiness to sin and shame (26). Within this range of connotations and meanings, no wonder red unsettles so many cinematic worlds in so many different ways.

In *Don't Look Now*, red moves and scintillates in a twilight zone of connotations: a color that seems to move even when carefully framed, so that a piece of clothing becomes a river of blood, becomes a passion whirling through the past or within the desperate sexual longings of a couple hoping to forget the past. Here red is about loss and passion, about disturbances of surface realities. Red is what happens beneath the liminal surface of water, when the unseen can radically disrupt the seen. No surprise that redfish are omnivorous, perhaps even in the canals of Venice.

In that somber and watery world of Venice and its slowly sinking churches, on the surface of the sinking city, red darts across the peripheries of vision, illuminating and shattering the watery calm that corrodes the ancient churches of a city haunted by a serial killer. While John, an architectural restoration expert, works to salvage a church there, Laura, still traumatized by her daughter's recent death, meets a pair of women who comfort her with visions of the supernatural, one blind who sees into the realm of the dead where, according to them, their dead child, Christine, wanders. Eventually, the suspicious John discovers his own version of Christine darting through the dark passageways of the city, a childlike body whose bright red coat flashes an impossible promise of redemption, a redemption running with blood.

The chilling opening sequence saturates the entire film, anticipating that narrative transition to Venice and the temporal and spatial dislocations that would galvanize the nightmarish collapse of this family. The heavy rains of a thunderstorm splatter a blue-gray pond, against which the title of the film appears, as the image zooms in on the rainy surface of the rippling water, sticks protruding from the apparently shallow waters. The opening credits start to roll: starring Donald Sutherland and Julie Christie, from a story by Daphne de Maurier, directed by Nicholas Roeg. A cut and then a vertical track up a seemingly abstract and dark image, across a pattern of small sparkling lights—is this is a blurred close-up of a church stain-glass window?—while the barely audible humming of a male voice is punctuated by the ominous tolling of a church bell. A difficult-to-see and unlocatable church window from another world, a homey hum, and a spiritually somber tolling within a layered image, already tinged at the start with a dark anticipation and lack of clarity about what is happening, what has happened, or what will happen. This will be a film about the perception of and through those layers—layers of the past and present, layers of the mind—introduced with the ironic warning not to look, or is it an imperative *to* look? "Don't Look Now!"

A childlike piano tune, almost as if being learned for the first time, becomes an intermediary sound bridge, introducing a young girl pushing a wheel barrel across a grassy and forested countryside, as a white horse gallops through the middle ground. (Doesn't that mythic white horse usually gallop toward a death, a disaster, another world?) So calmly bucolic yet bristling with edgy expectations. The small girl's bright red raincoat immediately stands out—no, leaps out—against the color-muted grass and trees, maybe a figure who does not belong in a surrounding natural world that begins to feel

strangely hostile. Then a cut to a young boy on his bicycle as he
carousels through a different, nearby part of the countryside. He
almost falls, with the last rays of the sun sinking in the upper left of
the frame. "Almost" emerges as a motif here: almost dead, almost
seeing. Crosscutting between the two children, the girl Christine
approaches with a toy soldier whose mechanical voice repeats re-
corded military commands. The war of surfaces and perceptions
has started. Disturbances ripple slowly between the sounds of that
innocent and childlike piano tune and the sharp but inaudible mechanical orders of the toy soldier. Christine retrieves a red and
white ball and, in an extreme low-angle medium shot, tosses it into
a nearby pond in front of her. A cut from the ball floating in the
water to a medium shot of Christine, the toy soldier still barking
his ominous orders and warnings. She crosses a narrow bridge
above the water. Then a crosscut to the young boy biking rapidly
through the woods, framed and obstructed by the limbs of trees.
Is he fleeing something? Christine bends over the water in front of
a large country home in the far background. A slow zoom tracks
down from Christine onto the surface of the water, before cutting to
a close-up of a blazing fireplace. A safe home, inside, above water,
reflecting comfort—but perhaps not.

A cut transitions to inside that home where the image pulls back
from a close-up of the blazing fireplace to a woman, Laura, who
reads in front of that fire, next to her husband John, an architect,
who examines slides of an ancient church projected on a screen before him, clearly the interior of a church with the now more identi-
fiable and dominant stained-glass windows above seemingly empty
pews, a church already sinking into the tides of Venice waters, a
church that John has been hired to pull from those waters, as a part
of a grand architectural reclamation and resurrection. I know the
enclosed sanctity of those stain-glass windows, as windows that
do not or cannot open to human perception, only the supernatural. Then, a close-up of Laura who reads in response to a question
that one of her children had once asked her: "If the earth is round,

why is a frozen pond flat?" Another cut to a low-angle shot of that large window in the slide, with the back of a small figure visible in a church pew in the foreground. This faceless figure wears a shiny red raincoat, which the image pans to, followed by a close-up of John whose interest has been, for some reason, piqued by this imagistic detail. He notices the figure and then inspects a different slide where he discovers a canted image of the same figure. Belatedly he responds to Laura, "It's a good question," indeed a perhaps a larger, paradoxical question about the natural world and the human perception of it that will reverberate through many more questions in the film and the disturbing limits of the look.

Water, fire, and ice entwine across these images. Shifting and connecting, they bear spiritual or symbolic meanings, no doubt. More fundamentally in this film, however, they describe transitions, transitions between epistemological substances, between the seen and the unseen, between the past and the future, between passion and restraint, between the natural and the supernatural, between life and death. As in so many of films in cinema history, the guide and pathway across those experiential zones is the color red, the color of two different Christs, a daughter and a savior, in John's secular church.

As the image zooms in on John's slide, there is a cut to the girl Christine running along the shore with the retrieved red ball, now inverted as a surface reflection in the pond. The boy accidentally rides across a glass pane on the ground, and the sound of the breaking glass somehow, impossibly, makes John, still inside the house, snap his gaze quickly from his work. Surfaces are beginning to shatter, spaces to collapse. Crosscuts between the two spaces of inside and outside the house are briefly interrupted by a longing glance from John toward Laura, a potentially emotional connection for the couple, except in this film passion ultimately only disconnects. In the realm of the everyday, a cigarette burns in an ashtray among dirty kitchen dishes. Laura then reads from a book the answer to her own question, explaining that the surface of a frozen lake can in fact curve, in one case as much as three degrees from the shore of one lake to other shore of that lake. To which John unwittingly summarizes the turbulence of those transitional surfaces that will define the rest of the film: "Nothing is what it seems." The alerted boy stops to inspect his tires for punctures.

A cut to a close-up of Christine, followed by a blurred close-up of the boy inspecting his tires with Christine in the far background poised over the pond in that red raincoat that unsettles almost violently the gray natural scene. The toy soldier's warnings continue to overlay the soundtrack. John retrieves his slides from the table, Christine tosses her ball into the water, John knocks over a glass of water that spills, in a close-up across one of the slides of the church interior, the ball spins on the surface of the water as the boy pulls the shards of glass from the bike wheel. Driven by unexpected disjunctive cuts, this is a film about puncturing and opening so many surfaces.

Then, through a magnifying glass, the spilled water spreads blood red from the red figure in the pew across the low-angled, close-up surface of the slide, like a viral amoeba crawling across the image, on the surface, beneath the surface, across the Christian/ Christine stain glass of no redemption. A close-up of John raising his head in some kind of troubled awareness, his eyes off left seeing the unthinkable outside the frame, as a cut reveals the boy racing across the lawn. "What's the matter?" Laura asks tensely. "Nothing," John responds as he darts out the backdoor. The fine line between nothing and something in this film. A blur of a dashing John crosscut with an overhead medium shot of Christine sinking slowly below the surface of the water; imagistic bubbles like those on the surface of a stain-glass window rise to another, watery surface. A long shot of John, already knowing and seeing, running frantically across the lawn, while the boy runs toward him shouting "Dad!" John runs clumsily into the water, breathing heavily, parting the surface of the water, not needing to search or to look. He knows, he has foreseen well before the blind visionaries arrives in Venice.

Waste deep in the pond, he pauses over the transparent wavering surface. Laura glances at a quick insert of a close-up of the stained slide, and then John dives beneath the water. A cut to a book on the couch, *Beyond the Fragile Geometry of Space*, followed by another close-up of the red smear, underscored by dark threatening music that grows louder through the scene, sliding across the image of the church interior. The horrifying fragility of space, surfaces, dividing lines.

In five fragmented overlapping edits of overhead shots, John rises in slow motion from the water, clinging to the dead body of Christine. He howls a preternatural scream. Another insert of the red blotch in the image linked now with the silent image of John, mouth agape with unspeakable despair. Red trails through the water as John raises the body to the surface, groaning as he slips and falls in the mud. Laura comes to the door, looks, and screams, an audial match cut links the scream to the sound of a drill, a drill exploring the watery wall of a compromised Venice cathedral. The fragile geographies of space and time. And my future in Venice.

8

Describing . . . Folds:
The Marriage of Maria Braun
(R. W. Fassbinder, 1978)

I once characterized R. W. Fassbinder's 1978 *In a Year of Thirteen Moons* as an "illegible" film in the sense that its formal and narrative densities resist and subvert the usual patterns and engagements that would allow the film to be traditionally interpreted and understood. With some significant flexibility and historical distinctions, that designation—as part of what I see as characteristic of a postmodern aesthetic—could apply to other Fassbinder films and to a range of other post–World War II films that in different ways reshuffle and subvert conventional interpretive stabilities and frameworks. Indeed, as I argued earlier about a broader shift in the writing of film criticism,

Describing Cinema. Timothy Corrigan, Oxford University Press. © Oxford University Press 2024.
DOI: 10.1093/oso/9780197625354.003.0009

the culturally traumatic watershed of the 1940s and World War II might be seen as a transitional period in which the stabilities of interpretation begin to erode and come under pressure. Within that erosion, the challenges and energies of critical description become, in turn, more and more prominent and problematic. That so-called illegibility in certain postwar films does not, in short, preclude description but may in fact foreground it as an increasingly necessary, difficult, and inventive response to a film, as a hermeneutical action that might successfully follow and engage those sometimes illegible textualities as less denotative descriptive mappings. What distinguishes Fassbinder's films, I think, is that those descriptive maps become specifically about the articulation of disjunctive and layered "folds."

I choose the word and concept of "folds" because folds replace the usual cinematic figures of logical sequentiality (such as narrative development) with a notion of overlapping simultaneity—so crucial to Fassbinder's claims about the legacy of World War II in contemporary Germany—where the past enfolds the present, often blindly, in a kind of simultaneity. Here I'm thinking of a dystopian and loose variation on Gilles Deleuze's use of the idea of folds (*The Fold*)—not, for me here, as a philosophical system but as a descriptive shape, an often graphic shape where interiority and exteriority, inside and outside, organic and inorganic, or the private and public enfold into each other, creating, for Fassbinder, a crisis of a self and a culture attempting to stabilize or locate themselves within the twisted and changing folds of ideology and economics, especially perhaps within the twisted materiality of habitat, place, and movie history. Moving through the fabric of draperies, clothing, rooms, sounds, and narratives, the eponymous protagonist of *The Marriage of Maria Braun* thus struggles to recognize that her inside is a compressed and changing fold of an outside where, as Deleuze says of the New German Cinema in general, spaces of self are continually "reduced to their own description" (*Cinema 2,* 136). Alongside Fassbinder's *Lola* (1981) and *Veronica Voss* (1982), *Maria Braun* is part of his BDR trilogy that, across those three films, enwraps three women's names and lives within fractured and drifting desires and identities played out through changing performative bodies, cinematic forms, historical moments, and the determining drives of consumer cultures within a postwar West Germany.

The plot of *Maria Braun* itself twists viewers through a series of melodramatic turns and returns. As bombs drop around the hasty marriage ceremony that opens the film, Maria and her new soldier-husband Hermann are immediately separated. While Maria at first assumes Hermann has been captured or killed during the war, he unexpectedly returns, takes the blame for her accidental murder of an American soldier, and is sent to prison. Awaiting his release in a distant future, Maria becomes both the business and sexual partner of the industrialist Oswald. Motivated by an *idée fixe* to restore her lost life with a husband, she works indefatigably to establish her utopian vision of a marriage that had lasted only two days, determinedly moving through the numerous collapsing mise-en-scènes of postwar German rubble culture, the U.S. occupation, and the economic miracle of the early 1950s, only to discover, in the conclusion, that these layers and frames have enfolded her into positions well beyond her knowledge or control, exposing her as a entrapped subject who, despite her controlling determination, is without a singular center or agency.

Throughout the final sequence of *Maria Braun*, Maria catches unsettling glimpses of this crisis, of herself sliding within the creases of those material layers that have been gathering around her throughout the course of the film. As she enters the house at the beginning of the sequence, she nonchalantly picks up a bouquet of roses from the front steps, their significance and sender strangely unimportant to her. Walking into the house, she casually places her purse in a vase filled with other dying roses she had previously received, an apparent ritual whose redundancy undercuts any symbolic or romantic meaning attached to the flowers. She immediately catches her mistake, however, in an oddly self-aware close-up, and she casually remarks, out loud to herself, on her fragile hold on the shifting objects, places, and materials that encase her life: "Maria Braun, don't start acting peculiar now," the clearly peculiar Maria smirks.

Following a cut, Maria slumps, bent over a table scattered with bottles of liquor and champagne, apparently drunk and passed out in her luxurious bourgeois home—whose exterior, glimpsed earlier, looks to me like a fortress—collapsed into herself, like a wealthy prisoner encased in a lifetime of booty. A pan reveals an interior of open doorways that create the multiple internal frames that become a claustrophobic maze of contiguous spaces. Here, junctures are also dis-junctures, creases between spaces that open and close around her. White, lacey drapes accent some passageways, dark wood panels draw in the walls of one room, and swirling, baroque wallpaper creates an atmosphere of suffocating excess. There's too much to look at here, surrounding the supine woman who envisioned it all.

In the hallway, next to the entryway, is a staircase that Maria will continually ascend and descend: a staircase as a traditional cinematic architecture, marking human aspirations, efforts, or desires (a symbolic architecture spread through movie history from Lang's shivering anticipation of fascism in *M* to Hitchcock's swirling vision of a postwar masculinity in *Vertigo*), a staircase that would become the back-and-forth vehicle of a confused, almost hysterical Maria. The center space of the floor is an open bedroom, positioned like a theatrical stage, anchoring a platform for sexual performance rather than a place of attainable rest in this world. Somewhere to the left of the frame is a kitchen, a barely glimpsed location of domesticity about to return as a kind of ferociously twisted repression.

Objects overwhelm this space with an abundance of materiality, a materiality that seems ironically to cover and envelop the surface of these spaces with a dense and elaborate presence. Rather than being enclosed within the places they inhabit, this material presence seems to pull the walls of the rooms in on themselves, physically disrupting the space as scattered and misplaced things.

Beginning with the wasted champagne and liquor bottles covering the table, the doorways and partitions of these rooms sag under the weight of flowing drapes that shroud the walls, while that richly patterned wallpaper pulls on those walls and oriental carpets and flowered vases create an atmosphere of fragile and claustrophobic exoticism. Even—or especially—a cigarette acquires a repetitive material weight. Maria retrieves one from her pocketbook (the first of two cigarettes that will become so much more than a realistic prop or even a measure of Maria's undercurrent of angst). She then enters the kitchen that, in a close-up of Maria lighting her cigarette, features only a gas stove with a brilliantly massive flame that she turns off after lighting her cigarette. Mirrors multiply images outside the kitchen: Maria regards herself twice in mirrors, examining the image she has created, and Hermann appears several times in a mirror in close-up, most dramatically when Oswald's revelatory will is read. From the start of the sequence, these mirrors begin to split apart both characters as though to mark the fault lines in this house of broken dreams.

Within this space, around these objects, dress measures movement; the covering of clothing becomes the agent of identity that links objects to characters, literally material folds within which Maria drapes, dresses, and transforms herself. Early in the sequence, there is a close-up of Maria's glowing face perfectly made-up, offset by her posh leopard-skin coat, over her elegant gray suit, and accented by a jaunty dark hat and veil: a star is born like a moving mannequin, like one of those naked props in Fassbinder's earlier *The Bitter Tears of Petra von Kant* (1972). Increasingly erratic on the edge of a quiet hysteria, hers is a body in trouble with the language of clothing. At one point she descends the stairs in lingerie and then haphazardly changes immediately into an elegant blue dress and later into a flowing white dress (unaware apparently of the difference between the inside and outside of her clothing), perhaps recalling her lost marriage. From lethargy to frenzy, movement mobilizes clothing within which Maria attempts, more and more desperately, to perform and orchestrate herself, as an increasingly distracted agent, a "Mata Hari of the economic miracle" as she calls herself. Like a crystallization of her entire life, the multiple temporalities, relationships, and materials that she has balanced and orchestrated for years begin to coalesce around her, like the fabric of a combustible history.

Suddenly, the lost but not forgotten Hermann appears at her door, having returned after his mysterious disappearance from a German prison years before. Stumbling to answer the doorbell, she opens the creaking door in a medium close-up, as if admitting an apparition into the house. Hermann Braun enters and almost violently embraces her as her stunned body folds into him like a lifeless puppet. He arrives in suit, hat, and tie, the blank public persona who, with his prison-time decision to sell his wife to Oswald, has vacated his own interior for a negotiated rebirth in wealth. But he too strips down to his underwear, still wearing the hat (a reference to Paul in Godard *Contempt*?), clothing as oddly uncoordinated as he and she are, a mismatch of private interiors and public exteriors. Displaced in this place of uncoordinated things, Maria will retrieve pajamas for him, the left-behind clothing of another, any man, as the insouciant Hermann wanders the room eating pre-packaged food from a can. Pre-packaged like they are.

Maria then moves rapidly across the spaces and interior frames from room to room, disappearing into the kitchen for a bottle opener, while Hermann sits in foreground eating. After earlier lighting that cigarette from the stove top, she later returns to light another cigarette from the same gas burner, which she then casually blows out, intentionally or forgetfully, releasing unseen gas, the gas of the camps—Unaware? Distracted? Intentional? As Maria and Hermann flatly discuss their mutual devotion and their marriage commitment, they move through the three planes of the central room, undressing. Wearing only her lingerie, Maria now lies across the bed seductively, while Hermann bends over hopelessly to embrace her and re-consummate, recover, return to their lost marriage and lost time.

Dialogue and sound surround and infuse the places and movements of the sequence with ironic, double-edged, broken, misdirected, and dislocating rhythms and meanings. Over the rapid buzz of a radio broadcast of the 1954 World Cup match between Hungary and West Germany, a staccato of overlapping phrases ricochet between the wife and husband: "Don't look at me like that until I'm ready," "I have to get to know you first, Mr. Braun. And when you remind me of someone I love very much, I won't need a dress anymore," "Maybe you should kiss your wife first. . . . After I finish this." As the camera slowly and almost suspiciously follows Maria and Hermann through these scattered phrases, each of them undresses, a movement that counterpoints a dialogue that again cracks with uneasy explanations and justifications about Hermann's disappearance, the wealth that each will consequently inherit, and the desire to offer each other new "contracts," confirming the financial contracts that have always enveloped their love and marriage, as the wallpaper of their emotions, contracts which will provide each other with all their separate possessions, a binder of overlapping pages, concluding with an inverted close-up of Hermann, who wraps the contradictions of their histories in paper-thin explanations: "I did it for you because I love you."

As Maria and the camera move around Hermann, the radio broadcast of the World Cup and the voice of announcer Herbert Zimmerman, with increasing volume, frantically attempts to keep pace with the action of the football match—and with the swirling layers of misaligned emotions engulfing the couple. The soundscape of the sequence shifts between the radio broadcast and the competing dialogue of Maria and Hermann about love and money, interchangeable backgrounds and foregrounds, overlapping different layers of desperate desire played out on a postwar turf.

"It's a goal, goal, goal!" Zimmerman screeches, as the sound of the doorbell rings, interrupting again the consummation of

their delayed marriage and announcing the forgotten arrival of
Senkenberg, Oswald's former assistant, and Mademoiselle Delvaux
to read the will of Maria's now dead substitute lover, Oswald; one of
many sounds that dramatically dislocate those circling movements
through this place, sounds that dramatically foreground the potential of cinematic sound to cross, permeate, invert spatial
boundaries, even dense folds, that they gather and remake.

A medium close-up shows the insouciant Hermann in a robe on
the bed as he turns to introduce himself and then cuts to a counter-
shot that zooms into a close-up of Senkenberg's face stunned by the
presence of Hermann. Delvaux reads the will that reveals the other
1951 contract, an agreement through which Maria was exchanged
between the two men, sending Hermann to Canada and allowing
Oswald to remain Maria's lover until his death. Realizing her place
as mere barter rather than secret agent, Maria exits the room, and
a close-up captures her running water over her wrist to calm the
shock of these different unimagined participants in the shared
fabric of her life. Hermann remains hunched in the back corner of
the bed. Maria returns for another cigarette and disappears into the
kitchen to light it. Suddenly smelling the invisible gas suffusing the
room, Hermann turns suddenly toward the kitchen, and screams
"No!" as the house explodes. In a counter-shot of the horrified
Senkenberg and Delvaux leaving through the outside gates of the
house, Delvaux screams and Senkenberg reenters the burning
house. The radio continues to blare the voice of Zimmerman on
the radio, whose screams within the rubble of the house folds 1951
back into 1945 and forward into 1979, enwrapping with caustic
irony those years into each other, inside out: "It's all over! Germany
is world champion!"

Throughout the last part of the sequence, actions and events rapidly shift and interrupt the sequence, pressing and colliding objects,
clothing, movements, and sounds against each other to create increasingly heated frictions and collisions. Just prior to this final sequence, when Maria explores the bombed-out shell of her former

school, she notes, "Reality lags behind my consciousness," and here the time zones of a postwar reality often lag, precede, and contradict both Maria's consciousness and the different layers of reality in the sequence. Most prominently throughout the sequence, personal and cultural memory, forgetfulness, and mis-remembering become figures of private and public histories specifically as asynchronous folds, of discontinuous moments that overlap or circle back on themselves as potential instances of revelation and insight but always too late or too soon to be recognized—from the remembered bombardments that open the film, to the final explosions that destroy Maria's house and life, to the coda sequence, at the end of the film, of de-realized negative photographs of the German chancellors from 1945 to 1979. Here, the different trajectories of Maria's home and life, like postwar German history for Fassbinder, collapse under the weight of a temporality that layers together then, now, and later, so that the difference between intention and accident becomes, in the end, moot.

9

Describing . . . Discretion: *Sunless* (Chris Marker, 1983)

If documentaries—traditionally, conventionally, supposedly— document a place, an event, a person, a time, then *Sunless* (*Sans Soleil*) seems to lyrically and aggressively scramble and disrupt those traditions and conventions. If describing documentaries might seem to be an act of reiteration, a recounting or measuring of the given realities of an event or a place, more or less transparently represented through objective perspectives and conventions, *Sunless* unmoors those traditional expectations and so shifts dramatically what there is to be described. Almost but not quite a travelogue, *Sunless* is less about places—ostensibly and primarily Guinea-Bissau and Japan—and more about, as the commentary claims, "a journey to the two extreme poles of survival." This

Describing Cinema. Timothy Corrigan, Oxford University Press. © Oxford University Press 2024.
DOI: 10.1093/oso/9780197625354.003.0010

documentary, or more accurately this essay film—travels to these and other places not as sites but as insights, engaging these places as reflexive meditations on conceptions of time and memory in the twentieth century, where extreme survival now describes a sphere, a climate, a zone in which the especially porous partition between life and death, presence and absence, create, a "poetry born of insecurity . . . moving in a world of appearances, fragile, fleeting."

Before the film begins it begins, muddling anticipation and suspense. At the start and then again at the end of the film: there is the grainy image of three children walking a road in Iceland in 1965, and the commentator, acting as the receiver and reader of letters from an absent filmmaker, recounts that filmmaker's effort to create a metaphor with this image, "He said that for him it was the image of happiness . . . and he has often tried to link it to other images but it had never worked." The image then transforms into an opaquely black screen before a cut to three U.S. fighter jets aboard an aircraft carrier, as the voice-over continues, over another black image, "One day I'll have to put it at the beginning of a film with a long piece of black leader. If they don't see happiness in the picture, at least they'll see the black." Within this rhetorically complex verbal and visual play, this image, all images perhaps but certainly images of happiness, totter on the edge of their disappearance, and, like the images of the children later to be lost in the black ash of a volcano eruption, their remembered presence can only be retrieved as a singular autonomous moment framed by the black of a leader and the black of a temporal passing, unconnected to and distinct from the world of other images that make up this or any other film or this or any other memory.

What logic or organization then holds a world of serial images and diverse global encounters together? For an answer, Marker's film turns, in a fascinating and almost whimsical way, to Sei Shonagon's eleventh-century *Pillow Book* of lists, which models the quest and project of the wandering cameraman in *Sunless* who pursues mostly or only "things that quicken the heart," a guiding motto, for me, for describing cinema, so different from Peter Greenaway's version of that same book as film, where a substantial body anchors and writes those fleeting images on its skin. At the intersection of the multitude of discrete memories and images of the world, Marker's film and its logic pose a different challenge, a challenge to locate and articulate these images in all their discreet and essential particularity as sounds and images on the frame edge of their continual disappearance.

"Discretion" is no doubt an odd word to associate with Marker's rigorous and complex *Sunless*, but I like the way it hovers between "discreet" and "discrete." To demonstrate discretion, as an overlapping of the two words, the film describes a way of looking back and a way of looking carefully at singularly distinct images, as a doubled action that acknowledges the autonomy of both sides of that exchange between those two ways of looking, between the haze of memory and the integrity of those images; namely, to acknowledge, without intrusion, the essential and specific otherness of disconnected and sometimes lost people, things, and the images they inhabit. Rather appropriately for the delayed work of describing cinema, I like the way Roland Barthes characterizes this kind of distanced engagement at the conclusion of his essay "Leaving the Movie Theater": "What I use to distance myself from the image—that, ultimately, is what fascinates me: I am hypnotized by a distance; and this distance is not critical (intellectual); it is, one might say, an amorous distance: would there be, in the cinema itself (and taking the word at its etymological suggestion) a possible bliss of *discretion*?" (349).

A world of discretion distinguishes "what is spoken or seen" from "what is left unsaid or unseen," allowing a combination of choice and discernment, noncontinuous distinction and unobtrusive prudence, a blissful serial of distinguished fragments and movements. Like the film's titular source in Mussorgsky's 1874 song cycle *Sunless*, discretion celebrates the many distinctive notes carefully orchestrated but separated as a composition of details moving through cycles of musical time. Perhaps this is what Carol Mavor, borrowing from Manny Farber (that champion of termite art and film descriptions), points to when she writes that *Sunless* "celebrates the infinitely small, as it chews and kisses its way through space like a tiny insect. With a bug's eye for detail" (96). Both Marker and Farber, the filmmaker and film critic, she continues, celebrate "an eye for chewing on meaning-laden chance detail, foraging space" (97).

How fitting then that this double articulation of discretion, in a space between the "discreet" and the "discrete," appears in *Sunless* first through that voice-over in which a female reads the letters from Sandor Krasna, a semi-fictional cameraman, an exchange and movement enacted across the uncertain distances between words written by Krasna, the aural reading of them by a woman in France, and the images on the screen. An uncertainty measured in the woman's commentary that both recounts, describes, and sometimes questions the words and images, it is a conversation and communication across the distance between faraway lands and Europe, a conversation full of wonder, curiosity, and poignancy. Through these various registers, discretion appears in the interstices that link and divide the seer, the speaker, and the world: in geographical gaps, in memory gaps, in the gaps between articulation and representations, between life and death.

A serial linkage of discrete things, rather than a narrative motivated by cause and effect, becomes the dominant organization that connects images across the gaps between them. Sometimes contrastive, sometimes cumulative, serialization is no doubt a standard pattern in many documentaries, but here it is as much about those spaces and gaps between the objects and people in that series. In this sense discretion in *Sunless* dissolves the ties of serialization. At one point in this global wandering, close-ups and medium close-ups of more than twenty faces of African women and men in Bissau appear. Earlier in the film, at a jetty in the Cape Verde Islands, a similar series of women and men, "patient as pebbles ... world travelers. ... a people of nothing, a people of emptiness, a vertical people," are introduced with a series of medium shots and a commentary that observes, while close-ups capture their direct and demanding stares—confrontational, nonchalant, bored, and amused—into the lens, these opportune and defiant looks back at the image, which seem to refuse voyeuristic eyes and gazes: "Frankly, have you heard of anything stupider than to say to people, as they teach in the film schools, not to look at the camera?" In this film, to look back is to claim autonomy, to arrest that serial movement, if only for a moment.

Later, on another dock, he, the unseen writer speaks through the voice-over reader, shifts the serial disappointments of history and revolution to a more immediate and salient question: "How to film the ladies of Bissau?" As medium close-ups scan the faces of these women, they dart away or shield their faces, waving away the film image, to be themselves. "Apparently the magical function of the eye was working against me," she reads, the image fixed on the back of a woman's head refusing to be exposed. Over the face of a young woman with a vibrant blue head scarf, the commentary observes that "it was in the market places of Bissau and Cape Verde that I could stare at them again with equality." A woman's eyes turn down and then up to confront the image, creating a back-and-forth movement that both acknowledges the image and rejects it: "I see her, she saw me; she knows that I see her." Traces of bodies cross between her face and the camera. Are these traces deflections or protections from the curious camera eye? "She drops me her glance," he and she continue, "but just at an angle where it is still possible to act as if it was not addressed to me." Then a reframed extreme close-up of her direct look above her slight smile, followed by a roll of her eyes—in amusement perhaps, in disregard for certain, as part of the game of discretion. Then the moment, a brief moment, in which the subject lives alone in the image: "Then at the end, the real glance. . . . Straight-forward that lasted a 24th of a second, the length of a film frame." Then she is gone, except as a trace of a film frame and the memory of it.

Discretion is of course based in acknowledged differences, gender always being a paramount difference. And so: there follows a montage of medium shots of several other market women, fully absorbed in themselves and in their work as they clean vegetables and decant oils in the open market, seemingly unseeing and uncontained by the world beyond that self and its work. "All women have a grain of indestructability," that far-off voice in France observes for her letter writer, a woman ventriloquizing a man's words, while one woman haggles firmly with someone off screen. "And men's task has always been to make them realize it as late as possible," the commentator explains, "but I wouldn't bet on the men." Another gap: pausing between the man with the movie camera and the woman with the voice, the faces of these indestructible women resist and persists.

Each body and face have their own restrained but determined expressions and shapes, and as the series accumulates one face after another, each shines forth with a distinctive and silent intensity: one stares, another turns away, one smiles, another glares hostilely, groups of women move baskets and sacks of grain and produce, a smiling child peers at the camera around the shoulder of a busy woman. Black faces surrounded by bright, blue, white, and red robes and head scarves, in motion, at work, self-contained and determined, beneath the hum of distant voices and conversations. Each is her activity, the work of survival. In a crowded space, a woman holding her baby, looks away left. Individuals, including men now, weave through a space full of bodies and the drone of inaudible conversations. A non-diegetic electronic beat and beep emerge against the hum of talk (drawing, I think, this world toward the computerized Zone that concludes *Sunless*, a site whose digital abstractions might hold discretion in suspense). Two young women, arms wrapped about each other turn their backs and walk away in a medium shot, alone and together. Another series of close-ups of utterly composed faces looking off and away from the image whose look they will not return. Someone's torso sorts potatoes or

turnips. Of course, a cat lounges in the sun, that mythically meditative emblem for Marker, whom I can imagine saying: Could there
be a more discrete animal than a cat whose entire posture and eyes
seem to say, "I am myself." The electronic beat goes on as silhouetted
men and women move stones along a human chain as some sort of
excavation or shoring up, a dance of work that ends in a medium
close-up of a playful and laughing woman in the center of the chain,
in the middle of the series: movements and transitions, retentions
and releases across the temporal and geographical gaps of survival.

While someone could imagine this sequence as a collective
representation of African men and women, almost a sampling of
types of faces and bodies like a modern August Sander's collection, I do not. Their specific places and movements in this series
is each their own, standing apart from any generalities that might
reduce them. They are not a continuous chain but the openings
within the harmonized series that connect them. As Marker puts
it in his photo-essay "The Koreans," "A market place is the Republic
of things"—that quicken the heart—where discretion wanders "as
a forgotten image between two shots" (39). This is magic Marker
in the market of the world: brightly and discretely highlighting
individuals, their cultures, and their histories in a way that always
allows you to see what you cannot see through that mark.

10

Describing ... Emplacements:
Do the Right Thing (Spike Lee, 1989)

In some films, certain sequences reach out, almost demanding a descriptive encounter as an entry or summary of that film. Like *Do the Right Thing*. Without any doubt, one of Spike Lee's most accomplished and formally layered films, it is also one of his most provocative films. Visible through its fictive tale in which Lee plays a pizza delivery man, Mookie, is an actual event that took place at Howard Beach, Queens, New York, where an African American man, Michael Griffith, died in a racially motivated attack in 1986. Underlining its historical and cultural backdrop, the film dedicates itself to other victims of racial violence (including Eleanor Bumpurs and Michael Stewart). With a theatrical structure that harkens back centuries to classical and neoclassical formulas for a dramatic unity of time and

Describing Cinema. Timothy Corrigan, Oxford University Press. © Oxford University Press 2024.
DOI: 10.1093/oso/9780197625354.003.0011

place, the events in the narrative occur within a single twenty-four-hour period and across a single Bedford-Stuyvesant neighborhood of several square blocks, a place and time where the blistering heat of a New York summer intensifies their classical compression and the intensely bright color scheme of the film. At the end of the day, that place and time explode in a senseless act of police brutality that lights the emotional fire of a furious riot that burns down Sal's Pizzeria, a riot provoked by Mookie's surprisingly decisive choice and action, an action so ambiguous that I find even careful description struggles to be certain of how and why it happens.

Place is habitable space, a crucial descriptive differentiation in this film where emplacement means taking an active social or ideological stance or position that transforms space into place. Where historical realism and ideological critique intersect in this film is in those places where Mookie travels and where he must negotiate the complex geography of a neighborhood spread through different races, generations, and economies: street life, gentrified blocks, an Italian pizzeria, generational dividing lines, a Korean grocery, Brooklyn stoops, and so on and on, all inflected by the power of images, sounds, and brands aiming to inhabit those places: all markedly identified by logos of sports teams and stars like Jackie Robinson and Larry Byrd, by boomboxes playing Public Enemy's "Fight the Power," and by the photos of famous Italians like Sylvester Stallone and Frank Sinatra. One of the many modern descendants of the nineteenth-century, Mookie is a flaneur who can wander through all spaces, a racialized version of Anne Friedberg's cinematic street walkers in her book *Window Shopping*. An irresponsible father and listless partner, Mookie slides smoothly across and through these different window frames and often contentious geographies, repositioning himself everywhere and nowhere, even within the family of Sal's racist sons, Pino and Vito, largely because he eschews any real position or committed agency in those spaces that he never inhabits. For the majority of *Do the Right Thing*,

Mookie is a sleepwalker through his own oneiric spaces that seethe with the intense heat of a blistering New York summer and a long cultural history of hometown colonization. Until, that is, he must "wake up" (as Mister Señor Love Daddy calls out in the opening, with his radio broadcast, reaching across the entire neighborhood) and must assume a stance along the most critical but perhaps least visible geographical border in the film (and across most American neighborhoods, I think): the line between public and private space where his eventually active emplacement between two spaces underpins the driving politics of the film.

The line that divides these two spaces wavers and falls apart in the penultimate sequence in the film. Just after Sal closes up shop and celebrates the financial success of the day, a group of neighborhood young men and women pound on the door asking him to reopen the pizzeria. Sal complies (to the dismay of his workers Mookie, Pino, and Vito), followed by a canted, extreme low-angle medium close-up of Radio Raheem (with his boombox blaring music), Buggin' Out, and Smiley entering behind the group and looking down at the scene; a scene now disrupted, out of balance, vibrating with sound through the crowded interior. As the shot pulls back, an overdue showdown erupts between alternate close-ups of Sal ("What did I tell you about that noise!") and the trio of young Black men ("We want some Black people on that mother fuckin' wall of fame now!"). A concentrated emplacement of the entire neighborhood about to become displaced: separated by the service counter, now a visible economic divide and barrier, Buggin' Out screams, "It's about the pictures!," and Sal screams back, "It's about the music!" Those are the pictures of famous Italian-Americans who adorn the walls of Sal's place, who brand the room under the imagistic markers of his financial ownership and his right to describe and inhabit the people and place he owns. (Aren't these images only the most prominent sign that in this world of images and the performance of them is where power resides?) Radio Raheem's music invades and breaks through the walls of the room and other barriers so that the voices and noises of the streets displace a place thought secure buttressed by an ideology of private property. It is a clash of racial economics: the consumers from the streets ride the wave of an aural fluidity and volume that flows from public space through the walls of private capitalism.

The force of sound now creates a spatial havoc: angry screams and racial insults intensify through a series of rapid crosscuts that include canted close-ups of Sal's sons, Mookie, and the neighborhood kids, infuriated, frustrated, fearful, and canted in a way that describes this space as a white economic sanctuary unbalanced and falling apart. As the visual and verbal attacks reach a peak, Sal suddenly smashes the boombox repeatedly with a baseball bat. He empties the room of sound and fills it with a lengthy and palpable silence, punctuated by Sal's breathless announcement, "I just killed your fuckin' radio" with the word "killed" resonating through not only the now silent space of the encounter and the subsequent space of the street but also beyond the film frame where white rage continues today to end more than just the life of a boombox. After that silent and extended pause and Sal's triumphant claim, Radio Raheem leaps over the counter— the counter that separates the power of the owner from the crowd he feeds—and drags Sal to the floor surrounded by a montage of screaming close-ups, searingly counterpointing a cut to images from Sal's speechless "Wall of Fame."

From the riot inside the pizzeria, the melee spills outside into the nighttime street where dozens of shouting neighbors swarm to the scene, surrounding the fight on the pavement where Radio Raheem chokes Sal. What starts inside, a purportedly private place, is now outside, chaotically public: inarticulate shouts, flailing arms, clashing bodies, and frantic faces. The police arrive, their bright blue uniforms standing out as the invasive colors of strangers in the darkened muted crowd. They drag Radio Raheem from the ground with a choke hold that lifts him off the ground. More inarticulate shouts between crosscut close-ups of Da Mayor, Mookie, Smiley, and others become desperate pleas to release the gasping Raheem, who dies in an extreme close-up that then cuts to his desperately shaking feet that could be the feet of a lynching victim decades ago. Eyes wide open but shut, Raheem lies dead on the ground in the foreground, while a cop kicks the body screaming "Get the fuck up!" Realizing what has happened, the police throw the body in their squad car and retreat frantically across the illusory line that once barely separated the history of African Americans from the future of George Floyd. The now handcuffed Buggin' Out shouts from another police car, and, as the infuriated crowd pursues the police cars, a close-up of Raheem's corpse on the floor of the car shifts upward for an eerie point-of-view shot out the back window at the pursuing crowd, a present pursuing the past. We see through the displaced eyes of the dead, the murdered, the past and future. As the squad car speeds away wailing with lights flashing, Smiley also wails with hands over his ears in the empty wasteland of an empty street. A slow pan from right to left across the stunned faces of neighbors rediscovering themselves in this moment, quietly articulating a refrain that goes on and on beyond the place of the frame and 1989 and 2023: "They killed Radio Raheem," "Just like Michael Stewart," "Murder," "They didn't have to kill the boy."

Moments later, the historical, political, and economic border dividing inside and outside, private and public, graphically appears, a now fully visible border, strained to a breaking point. A close-up of Mookie turns to Sal also in close-up, both poised tensely in front of the pizzeria with the two sons. A reverse shot shows a group of neighborhood men lined up across from them, also still and tense, glaring across that line. Mookie slowly crosses over, leaving and re-placing himself with a different self, leaving a shaken Sal to say what he can only say in a situation that offers nowhere to hide on the street: "Do what you gotta do." That imperative hangs fire, fraught with ambiguity. Da Mayor pleads for calm: "Somebody's goin' get hurt. . . . We're going to regret this." But what is "this"? The loss of life? The destruction of a building? Of a neighborhood? The accusations accelerate while a counter-shot pans the strained and resigned faces of Vito, Pino, and Sal: back and forth across that dividing line, the temperature of an already overheated day tangibly rises across this fraught geography.

Once a modern flaneur drifting through space, Mookie now decides to not simply wander between spaces but to move against a society of confrontational, repressive emplacements. Staring off at the scene, he slowly drags his hands down across his face and then holds them over his mouth and chin in a medium close-up describing, a most important detail I believe, a difficult thought in action. A cut to Mookie shows him then walking deliberately to a trash can, tossing aside the bag inside, and then briskly returning— again deliberately—to the pizzeria (so deliberately in fact that it certainly not an act of passion but a movement of thought). As he throws the garbage can through the front window, he yells, "Hate!," which echoes back through the film and forward to the closing quotations from Martin Luther King Jr. and Malcolm X, a dialectical dialogue that Smiley offers throughout the film with his photographs of the two Black leaders and that Raheem wears with brass knuckles imprinted with Love and Hate. (Does the reference to the 1955 *Night of the Hunter* make Raheem a modern preacher like the demonic Robert Mitchum whose hands are tattooed with the same words?) As the garbage can crashes through the picture window of the pizzeria, a doubled overlapping edit shows the can smash through the window first from the perspective of the street and then again from inside the pizzeria. Without the illusory separation provided by that window, the interior collapses into the exterior, the place of the private now within the public.

The sequence and Mookie's action become a flashpoint of meaning and intention (which Lee has not helped clarify with his usually evasive comments). Intense anger about Raheem's death? Or a calculating redirection of that fiery anger directed at property instead of life? I like the latter. Directorial intention is, I believe, overrated, perhaps never lucid and singular, and certainly not either for Mookie or Lee. As the crowd storms inside the pizzeria, the subsequent destruction is not simply revenge. As the images and editing capture the chaotic action violently out of control—furniture destroyed, cash register emptied, objects thrown into the street, a fire started—the emplacement of private property becomes displacement and replacement of the burning images on the Wall of White Italian Fame. Amid the strange celebration, a slow pan across the stunned and vacant faces of Sal and sons. In the smoldering rubble, with the mesmerizing lyrics of "Fight the Power" weaving through the debris, Smiley pins a photo of Martin Luther King Jr. and Malcolm X on the ashes of the wall, and he smiles. The stuttering Smiley, a wiseman of history, replaces history.

Later, in the burned-out wreckage of the pizzeria, now an uninhabitable place, a place whose economics and politics begin to rise from the morning ash and trash in the street as a now actionable place. The voice-off of Mister Señor Love Daddy sounds through the neighborhood: "My people, my people what can I say? . . . Are we goin' live together? Together are we goin' live? . . . Today's weather Hot!" The shot cuts to and then zooms in on an extreme close-up of the sleeping Mookie. Love Daddy shouts, "Wake Up!" to bring the narrative full circle, but now Mookie has been finally "woke," as a new day begins, even forecasting new political days twenty years from 1989. He leaves his young son and rightfully annoyed partner, Tina, to retrieve his back pay from Sal. A tracking shot follows Mookie as he marches briskly to confront Sal bent in despair in the doorway of the charred frame of the blackened remains of the pizzeria, now a space barely distinguishable from the trash in the streets. Temporarily, so much for capitalism.

Their exchange is sharp and pointed: Mookie wants his pay; they trade bitter accusations about Radio Raheem's death and who caused it; Sal vents about the loss of his building as a place now in ashes; Mookie dismisses this romance of property by pointing out that the insurance company will reimburse him; and Sal responds by angrily throwing five crumbled hundred-dollar bills at Mookie, Sal mocking Mookie's new riches. More haggling face to face, they

argue in a low-angle medium shot over the crumbled bills between them and the argument about who should pick them up.
After some quiet words of mutual concern, Mookie picks up the
money, announcing he has to see the son and the partner whom
he has avoided since the start of the film. Is this a new sense of responsibility for the irresponsible flaneur? For me it is no small moment: not only does it suggest the discovered place of responsibility
in this tremorous public landscape and in Mookie's own personal
life, but it is also, I think, an important extra-filmic moment: the
woke Mookie is now aware of what the Hollywood filmmaker Spike
Lee has learned and made part of his career. Whether a gig worker
or a celebrated auteur, representation, power, and agency are driven
by capital leverage. You can pick up the money and make it a force
for personal and social change.

As Mookie walks through the scarred streets of the previous eve-
ning, the prospects of that responsibility continue to expand beyond a single place or a small neighborhood into the larger public
sphere, mobilized by the voice-off of Love Daddy, whose omnis-
cient overview now urges a political action that might replace the
mere loss of private property with the larger issues and within the
larger place of community action: "I see you Mookie," he says, "Go
home to your kid." Beyond Mookie, beyond his home, beyond
Bed-Stuy, the radio sound of Love Daddy points to a broader and
more powerful place for action: "Register to vote! The election is
coming up."

11

Describing . . . Noise: *The Piano*
(Jane Campion, 1993)

Even during the silent era, noises have been an everywhere dimension of the film experience beyond the film itself: noises in and
outside nickelodeons, noises of loud projectors whirling, noises of
annoyingly chattering audiences. Within films themselves, there are
likewise many kinds of noises: some are external to the story on the
screen, some internal within it, or to use filmic terms, some noises
are diegetic with a source in the image, some non-diegetic with no
source in the image, and some internal diegetic whose source may
be the internal thoughts of a character. Most films orchestrate the
first two, and many films integrate all three. But few films focus so
strategically and creatively to expand and remix all three to make a
film provocatively centered on kinds of sounds and noises as Jane
Campion's *The Piano* does. In this, I assume a somewhat contrarian
view, since for me *The Piano* is not just or even primarily about the

Describing Cinema. Timothy Corrigan, Oxford University Press. © Oxford University Press 2024.
DOI: 10.1093/oso/9780197625354.003.0012

pervasive piano music of the title that links the mute Ada to the social world around her. Rather, across its elaborate soundscape, the film explores, most importantly I'd argue, the noises that fluctuate between silence and music: the noise of water and mud pulling the self into the earth, the noise of an axe sharply chopping pieces of the earth and pieces of people, the noise of a material of culture, including its music, breaking into atonal fragments.

A nineteenth-century presumably widowed woman, Ada McGrath, travels by ship from Scotland to New Zealand with her young daughter, Flora, for a bartered and arranged marriage to a man she has never met, Alisdair Stewart. From the opening moments in the film, barter already reduces the human, its social values, and its central ritual of marriage, to material transactions, made all the more exploitative in this marriage by Ada's lack of power and voice. Ada's piano and its music—a large unwieldy object through which she transcends her limitations and her culture, with a melodious classical score so seemingly incongruous in this wilderness on the other side of the world—concentrate the surging emotions and sensualities that pulsate through the drama. Although Ada has chosen (or did she?) to be mute since she was six years old (or so we are told), the film paradoxically begins with her voice-over explaining that "the voice you hear is not my speaking voice; it is my mind's voice." That internal voice, inside her mind, describes a silent, imaginary realm, unheard by others, which finds its visual corollaries in stunning overhead crane shots of a fantastically composed other world, maybe the perspective of angels who later would come to earth in the pageant-play costumes of Flora and others, images, like the music, not entirely of the earth, not entirely human. To the world outside her mind, to that other world of human beings, Ada speaks only through the music of that piano and through sign language communicated to her young daughter, a sign language, by the way, whose articulations are often made explicit by the eruptive noises of Ada's slapping hands and fingers.

The noise I hear in *The Piano* differs from more codified sounds or sound effects in most movies, where those sounds function as formal articulations like speech, or atmospheric music, or the controlled integration of so-called ambient sounds providing background information about the setting. In those cases, the sound of noise, such as a car horn honking or a telephone ringing, may simply serve realism or, as in David Lynch's films, a kind of surrealism. Usually, these noises serve specific narrative functions that explicitly serve to help define characters, their situations, their human motivations, and their story. Noise in these films rarely becomes a violation or an intrusion in a way that would counter actions or meanings at the forefront of the narrative, intrusions that the evolution of sound technology has consistently sought to reduce or control, by carefully producing what film technicians call, with some irony here, ambient "wild" sounds added to merely thicken the background of a movie. A crack of thunder might announce a threat to a character alone in the wilderness; the screeching of urban traffic places a sensitive character in a dangerous environment; the clanging of a trolley might beckon young lovers to climb aboard.

In *The Piano* intrusive noises are everywhere: inimical, unwanted, unexpected, incongruous, or perhaps indifferent forms of nature that periodically drown out, submerge, and silence the sounds of a fragile culture and fragile people, cultures and people who struggle to contain, domesticate, or colonize those incomprehensible noises. (Wasn't it Werner Herzog who said in a different jungle that "the trees here are in misery, and the birds are in misery. I don't think they sing, they just screech in pain"?) From the beginning of the film, these noises merely trouble the narrative, but they quickly gain amplitude and significance through their recurrence. In *Noise Matters*, Greg Hainge describes noises in David Lynch's *Eraserhead* (1977) in a way that might—with many qualifications—apply to *The Piano*: as noise "that pulls meaning away from apparently fixed forms back towards a brute materiality or pure expression which is to say an expression that exceeds any attempt at synthesis, suture or exegesis" (179-180). I read somewhere that these aggressively material noises can "colonize" the film's manifest narrative content. How on the mark then to say that the reckless noise in *The Piano* recolonizes the colonial empire at the center of this film.

In the opening sequences there is the noise of Flora's roller skates clanging down a hallway in Scotland; shortly thereafter is the dominant rhythmic noise of oars stroking loudly through the water as Ada's ship arrives in New Zealand; then there is the clamor of incomprehensible voices struggling to land her boat on shore, amidst the crashing of turbulent storm waves and the angry slaps of Ada's hands as she signs her disgust with the sailors; afterward, the native Maori chatter vociferously as part of the noise of the jungle; and then there is (especially) the sucking sound of the feet as they move from the beach to the homestead, slogging through thick mud in which Ada's Victorian boots and skirt sink into and then struggle to pull free of that watery mud. All this in the opening moments of the film. Later, noise fractures the soundscape as the continual pounding splatter of sheets of rain, the irritating creaking of the floorboards in the rustic houses, Ada's violent ripping of the lace from her wedding gown, the sharp splitting noise of an axe chopping wood, and the eruptive smashing of teacups. In this noisy environment only music keeps humanity barely afloat, piano music that is, though, increasingly dissonant toward the end of the film, sharp and aggressive, as it assimilates the noise of this environment. No wonder that, for the cultural guardians of this outback, for those tongue-wagging matrons and selectmen, even Ada's piano playing seems like no other music, sounds "strange," a marginally human music.

Let's remember that the English word "noise" has its etymological source in the Latin and old French words for "nausea," usually associated with seasickness. How appropriate then that this film and its cacophonous environment of unwanted "bruit" begins with

Ada's seasickness and almost ends the film with her transformative drowning in those same waters.

In *The Piano*, barter produces noise. Landing on the shores of a New Zealand wilderness, with the piles of heavy baggage and that cumbersome piano, thick Victorian clothing, and tightly bound gender codes—the misplaced leftovers of a far-off Europe—she meets her new husband and quickly discovers a world of barter in which she has already been a piece of property in a marital exchange, the barter of woman as a thing: a barter like the noise of those chopping axes as trade tools to control indigenous lands and people, a barter like George Baines, the Westerner gone native, dismantling Ada's piano, purchased with Maori land he has bought, to exchange pieces of it back to her for physical intimacy. And then climactically: the barter of a human finger for a prosthetic finger with which to replay the piano. The human becomes a material, a physical thing, to be exchanged for other physical things, and in that exchange—as with so many bartered objects in the film—the collision between an imaginary value and real sounds produces often disruptive clashes of noises. Recall the odd but revealing humor of the Maori men mistaking a shadow-mime production of *Bluebeards Castle* for actual physical violence and then charging the stage through a chorus of screams. Within this world of barter, the subsequent noise replaces social sound—as inarticulate, uncivilized, unrecognizable—as a harbinger of death.

This drama of noise crescendos when, dressed in her costume as a covering cherub brought to earth, Flora begins a late sequence as the child-mother of her mother-child, Ada. Throughout the film Flora has been the voice of Ada's silence, the inverted mother to her silent child, her guide and interpreter. Now, as Flora washes doll clothes for her fantasy family outside their cabin, Ada asks her to deliver a piano key to Baines, on which Ada has written a short note professing her undying love for him. That swelling piano music that had accompanied Ada when she arrives on the tempestuous and isolated beach in New Zealand returns, as she forces her resisting daughter to carry the message to Baines. In a medium long shot, Flora skips across the rickety boards that form a precarious walkway through the ubiquitous mud and among the charred, barren trees. Suddenly, however, she changes directions at a crossroad between violation and civilization, and she splashes through the muddy water to the other fork in the path, now determined to show the note to Stewart, not Baines. A low-angle canted medium shot follows her as she sings and dances toward the betrayal, followed by a long shot of her scampering across the empty hills in the distance. Why canted? A visual earthquake, or at least slippage, within the social order, opening noisy fissures? In a medium shot, she climbs a hill along fence posts toward her stepfather, who pounds, rhythmically, loudly, and auspiciously, new posts in the ground, barriers and sounds of control and colonization. As she hands him the key with its misdirected message of passion and love, Flora assumes her inverted family position: "Mother wanted me to give this to Mr. Baines. I thought it not the proper thing to do." Another low-angle canted medium shot as Stewart reads the message, and a similar canted image follows him down the hill, ferociously seeking vengeance. His Maori workers curiously watch the scene, picking up the discarded piano key and attempting to create the sound of the piano by tapping it, but only hearing dull thuds: "It's lost its voice. It can't sing," they prophetically comment in their native language. Ada too is about to lose her singingly silent voice.

The thematic music associated with Ada rises again on the soundtrack, as a non-diegetic sound pervading a world of imaginative longing, now more poignant than previously as it anticipates Ada's own violent departure from that world. Stewart and Flora race in separate cuts through darkened woods suffused with a blue glow, as they splash through those muddy swampy waters, a drowning noise competing with the ethereal musical soundtrack, almost drowning it out, a noisy submergence of the anticipated violence signaled in a close-up image of Stewart's axe, the colonial axe whose noise has punctuated the entire film. Flora spins in disorientation. A cut to a medium shot of Ada as she looks off-screen, suddenly aware and frightened, as Stewart bursts into the room. He tosses Ada onto a table and then drives his axe into the piano frame, a sharp splintering noise in close-up. "Why," he screams, "I trusted you!," and he ferociously tosses her onto another table scattering the spools of thread, with more loud breakage and clattering of the remnants of social niceties.

A thunderous storm rages over the music as he drags her into the muddy yard, while she fights frantically and hopelessly to escape. Yelling "do you love him?," he pulls her arm onto a tree stump and brings the axe down with an explosive bang on a finger of her hand. Flora screams hysterically "Mother," calling her by that familial name for the first time in the film. Is this the grotesque moment when this inverted mother-daughter relationship crosses for the first time into a recognizable social order, where silence and fantasy give way to that order and its language? "I clipped your wings," Alisdair would later say to Ada, this other fallen angel who has now fallen fully into the noise of the world. She stumbles to her feet, with a blank catatonic stare, wavers unsteadily through the sea of mud, shrinking partly to her knees engulfed in the watery dark surface and sounds.

In the end: leaving New Zealand with Baines in a Maori canoe, precariously balancing the rocking piano in rough seas, Ada is pulled under (again) into the watery noise of the ocean that, as she sinks under its surface, returns her to silence. She and her piano drift deeper and deeper into this underwater sea, a return to a noiseless grave. Surprisingly, for her and for me, she suddenly refuses that grave, frees herself from the piano, and swims to the surface, resurrected and integrated back into the world, where she later will begin to speak with rough articulations and will begin to play a different music: the music of a rediscovered humanity, seen and heard in the bartered metallic prosthetic finger that replaces her lost finger, an emblem perhaps of a kind of physical disfigurement that, in different forms, has marked so many tragic figures since Oedipus and Lear as they painfully discover their lost humanity. The intrusive clicking of that finger on the keys of the piano becomes different, a sensual sound, a version of "a weird lullaby" that she has pulled her into and back from the silence of the ocean floor, a harmonic but scarred sound, composed between the music of her silence and the inhuman noises of the world whose eventual acceptance and integration defines humanity.

12

Describing . . . Interiors: *A Taste of Cherry* (Abbas Kiarostami, 1997)

Abbas Kiarostami's *Taste of Cherry* opens inside the car of Badii as he drives through streets lined with laborers who hope to be offered work. His gaze moves intensely across the different faces outside, searching those faces for something that has yet to be named. Any speculation as to what he is looking for at this point is impossible. Anticipating Kiarostami's later 2002 film *Ten*, which explores the lives of ten women in ten different vignettes, each conversation is usually enclosed within an automobile, the interior as a space dramatically separated—socially, psychologically, physically—from the street activity that passes outside the car window, an interior only occasionally interrupted in *Taste of Cherry* when laborers approach to ask for work, in a series of terse shot/counter-shot exchanges.

Describing Cinema. Timothy Corrigan, Oxford University Press. © Oxford University Press 2024.
DOI: 10.1093/oso/9780197625354.003.0013

(Later the empty countryside would fly by, likewise in stark contrast to the conversations within the car's interiors.) More than a conventional formal distinction between a conversational foreground and background, this graphically isolated interiority becomes the space of Badii's tormented self, enclosed and separated from the exterior world around him, a virtually unknowable interiority, containing his unclear motive for that suicidal quest that is soon identified as his motive, a desperate interiority, in which he desires not only to die but also to be doubly enclosed, buried by a stranger inside the earth, to be encased under the ground that moves outside around him. Especially in this film, describing what that interior may fully be seems necessarily and perhaps uselessly speculative. Speculative description? A description of a negation or a negative space? Punctuated no doubt with multiple "maybes" and "possiblies."

As he leaves Tehran, Badii drives through the surrounding arid brown and yellow hills on a winding dirt road, seen often through high-angled long shots that suggest the still winding ways of his fatal decision, as he searches for an unknown accomplice who will return with him to his chosen gravesite. Along those roads, he first picks up a young hitchhiking soldier, and so begins a series of tightly circumscribed conversations within the car between Badii and the soldier and later with two other men who eventually join him in the front seat of the car: besides the timid Kurdish soldier, an Afghani seminarian visiting a friend, and finally a Turkish taxidermist who works at a local museum, all join him in his car. Through face-to-face counter-shots, each encounter produces extended discussions that gradually reveal Badii's strange request but not his motivation: to have someone return the next morning to an open grave in which he will likely—but not certainly—have committed suicide with sleeping pills. He offers each of his riders a large financial reward for covering his body with earth—if he should be dead. That all three men represent Persian minorities in Iran suggests their own marginal place, as culturally divided or alienated subjects, and each conversation with Badii highlights a different outsider's perspective on Badii's determined but mystifying intent to kill himself: mystifying for one, it is an act frightfully beyond a fundamental social behavior; for another it is a morally misguided affront to a spiritual world; and for a third a failure to perceive the sensual delights and human pleasures found in the natural world—like the taste of cherries.

The prelude to the second encounter with the seminarian develops and details a particularly subtle movement between those interior and exterior spaces that structure the entire film. As Badii continues to wind his way through the mostly barren hills, at one point he stops to stare at a group of soldiers chanting and jogging in formation on a lower road, soldiers who will reappear later in the film. He then passes laborers working on the hillside, and after accidentally running his car off the road, a group of those workers cheerfully push his car back onto the road. These men are a community, a group with a purpose, far from Badii's enclosed self, far from his terminating desire to be off the road.

Back on that windy road to what will probably end only with his end, he approaches a cement plant located in a largely empty and arid landscape, where he discovers a security guard who is the lone occupant of a small watchtower amidst deserted buildings. After greeting the guard, who sits off-screen above him, Badii asks if he is alone, which begins a threaded motif about "aloneness" in the sequence, as if Badii needs on some level to examine, question, and reflect on his own isolation in the world outside him, to find perhaps other sympathetic loners, other narcissistic confirmations of himself. At this point the guard invites him to climb a ladder to join him for tea. Will this hut, a place above the ground and the earth, provide perspective or even clarity on that earth that inexorably appears to draw him below its surface? The small, dirt-brown, elevated hut has a balcony with plants, on which the guard sits making his omelet in front of a room surrounded by large glass windows on all sides. A transparent interior suffused by an encompassing, empty, exterior.

Their conversation turns, almost casually, to the dust and earth covering the outside and enclosing them inside, dust and earth, for Badii that final human interior, that final enclosure. "What a nice a place," Badii says, while looking off into the distance with a kind of longing. "Nice? It's nothing but earth and dust," the guard replies, knowing the terrain but not, as Badii does, the dark promise of that terrain. Speaking on the balcony from outside the enclosed room with words that speak a different inside, Badii counters: "You don't think earth is nice? Earth gives us all good things." The perplexed and literal-minded guard responds: "So according to you all good things return to the earth." For Badii, speaking elusively as usual, the earth not only gives but also takes all good things—including himself.

As the guard rises to make tea, in a medium shot, Badii peers off the balcony into the distant sky, the guard still visible through the glass windows in that transparent interior. Increasingly, this conversation with the guard seems to act as a stand-in for Badii's oblique dialogue with his own self, his unexplained need to kill himself, and his anticipated burial in the earth. The conversation becomes a self-reflection through the windows of his own isolation, a glimpse of that nameless negation inside him.

A cut follows Badii's eyeline, fixated now on a hill above him where a bulldozer dumps a large load of rocks and dirt down the hillside, releasing clouds of brown dust. A reverse medium shot from the interior of the glass windows of the observation room shows Badii watching as the earth slides down the hill, staring in a longish take as the rocks spill down toward him in the background, almost seeming to fall over him, a covering landslide of earth tumbling toward his precarious self, burying it hopefully by morning, in mourning. He turns back toward the room and asks the guard if he ever gets bored amidst so much desolate earth, to which the guard replies, "I'm used to it. I'm used to loneliness too." Is it loneliness or boredom that drives Badii, or maybe it is a suffocating combination of the two? Against the background of the brown rocky hill overlooking the building, almost like high walls or the inside of a tomb, Badii wanders around the corner of the balcony, pacing in thought—about his own state of nonbeing, no doubt. From the balcony, he asks the guard inside if he knows the man he sees off-screen in the distance, as his voice grows nearly inaudible in the exchange. The guard answers that the man is his Afghan friend, a seminarian visiting him while on holiday, a friend who is also lonely. Badii walks back and forth outside the windows, rubbing his hands together in vexed thought. "I didn't catch what you said," the guard says in reply to the mumbled comments of Badii behind the glass. Badii is a man barely audible to anyone other than to his own tormented self, while he continues to pace back and forth, looking off in thought. About his isolation, about his boredom, about his plan.

(Earlier in the sequence, the guard notes that there are many Afghans living in Iran, fleeing the war in their own country. Badii counters that there is also the current war between Iran and Iraq. "Your war doesn't concern us," only "troubles us," the guard answers. The Afghan war, he explains, "was harder, more painful for us." About which I wonder: Why so many soldiers and wars across this existential landscape? Earlier the young soldier prompts Badii to comment on the violence and wars suffered by the Kurds, and, both early in the film and later, there are those soldiers who jog in formation along the dirt road in the distance. On the edge of this world there is constant warfare or potential warfare it seems, an exterior always on alert, always about inevitable death and dying. Another speculation without clear designation or certainty.)

Badii continues to pace the balcony outside, agitated. He asks why the guard is here alone on a holiday and tries once again for a bond, for a recruit for his death pact: "You feel sad. So am I." Turning the corner and reentering the room, he invites him, coyly, to go for a ride "to get a change of scenery, talk." But the guard refuses: "It's my duty. We all have responsibilities," unwittingly taunting Badii who may or may not have responsibilities but who is now probably well beyond any responsibilities toward one person or a social and communal world. Exiting onto the balcony where the dialogue is once again muted, he continues his search, saying: "I'll go see your friend the seminarian." He climbs down the wobbly ladder and leaves through the rusting machinery around the cement plant to find that other interlocutor for whom he will again reveal his incomprehensible interior. The windowed space of the hut transparently opening to the outside, the dialogue moving in and out of audibility, and Badii's vague determination, all wobbly, all collapsing inside.

Later, in a long shot from a distance, Badii returns to an apartment, seen only as small barely lit window frames of its interior. Where he is now is not quite clear, another unseen interior, whose inside can only be vaguely implied. In that long shot of the apartment, the window light turns off as Badii leaves to disappear into the night on his way to the open tomb—or not—which the film image anticipates with a virtual blackout of the image as rain on the soundtrack refreshes the scorched earth with the vague possibility or impossibility of renewal.

In the often questioned and commonly criticized coda of *Taste of Cherry*, the film pulls back unexpectedly from the story of Badii to a metafictional space outside the fictional frame of the film. Now, videotape footage replaces the celluloid film to record Kiarostami directing that group of marching soldiers in the distance through a phone, while actor Homayoun Ershadi playing Badii walks in the foreground, relaxed, smoking a cigarette, and observing the filming apart from him, neither inside nor outside. From nowhere, there is the sound of Louis Armstrong playing a jazz trumpet classic, "St. James Infirmary," a dirge about death that also carries within it a muted celebration of life under its somber melody. That binary of cinematic interiors and exteriors that haunts Badii throughout the film gives way to a different spatial configuration made possible by that different visual medium of videotape, so that the dramatic and conflictual spaces of filmic interiors and exteriors, describing vague encounters between pasts and futures, gives way to the preparatory space of a videotape present, immediate and re-doable, a space of unknown and indeterminate potential to replay. Across the shift from celluloid to video, *Taste of Cherry* closes, in short, with an opening: for a few minutes exiting that morbidly claustrophobic interiority of the narrative to enter an open-ended profilmic space, both outside and inside the frames of Badii's story. As Laura Mulvey describes it, the coda offers "a possible resurrection and return, phoenix-like, from the ashes" of the film's narrative (143). Or, in terms that respond more pointedly to my description here, Stanley Kauffmann writes in an early review that, with the coda for the film, "a quiet spaciousness begins to inhabit it" (73).

13

Describing... Correspondence:
Central Station (Walter Salles, 1998)

Rio de Janeiro's Central Station is an expansive terminal overflowing with constant movement and redundancy, anonymous
crowds, descending in waves from arriving trains and ascending
onto departing trains, through the barely comprehensible chatter
of public announcements. Petty thieves are summarily executed
without questions or debates, houseless vagabonds silently search
through the garbage. In this bustling place of whirlwind activity,
Dora writes letters to the loved and lost for her illiterate clients,
for the angry, the forlorn, and the desperate, people who can
speak their hearts but not write the words in letters, letters that
she promises to send but which the cynical Dora never actually
does. Like the unsent letters, the overheard conversations in this
central station linger suspended in the spaces of change, desire,
and regret. A road film, a coming-of-age film, a commonly seen
narrative about a son in search of a father, *Central Station* is not
only about letter writing as a vehicle of hope but also more largely

Describing Cinema. Timothy Corrigan, Oxford University Press. © Oxford University Press 2024.
DOI: 10.1093/oso/9780197625354.003.0014

about the material fragility of words as a correspondence between people, where to correspond means to connect across the chasms of human need and difference, across distance, time, age, and suffering. Words in letters and letters of words are the obvious correspondences in *Central Station*, but correspondences through the film also describe the movement between two kinds of existence: as lost and as found. As in some airports around the world, "correspondences" are passageways between flights, within travel. Here I dare to think of myself as the first person to find in this film the angels of Emanuel Swedenborg, the eighteenth-century theologian, whose philosophy of spiritual correspondences between the human and the spiritual realms takes different flight in a road movie that appropriately begins in a transportation center. After all this is a film essentially about the discovery of spirit and the spiritual in a human domain, but unlike those vertical correspondences of Swedenborg between the two levels of the human and the spiritual, in this film correspondences are horizontal and multiple, materialized as letters, as a physical exchange, as crumpled and discarded papers in a desk drawer, making Swedenborg's model strangely concrete and social, subject in this modern world to a capitalist realm of economic exchange.

This is first a tale of communication and compassion, both of which, especially in this film, materialize through words— words written, spoken, unsaid, misunderstood. Dora first encounters nine-year-old Josué when his mother, Ana, asks her to write a letter to the father that her son, Josué, has never met. Shortly after, Ana is killed, a tragically incidental event on these mean streets of Rio, by a bus outside the station. After this Dora reluctantly tries to find a home for the boy, and later she grudgingly joins him in a search for that lost father through the countryside of Brazil. A former schoolteacher who has retreated bitterly from the world, she personifies a minimal vocabulary of negatives ("No children, no husband, no family, no dog"), surviving through the business of writing faux correspondences that will never be sent or read, thus corresponding to nothing. Without family, Josué is reticent and recalcitrant, responding with angry stares into the world in front of him. Inaudible communications resound through the station off-screen, waves of hostility and suspicion connecting mute eyeline exchanges, curses filling the air of Rio as the odd companions flee on a bus journey across the countryside of northern Brazil. On the bus, she explains words to him as a way to mark and distinguish experiences along different linguistic planes: the difference between taking a "taxi" and a "bus" or what different "fathers" look like as visual signs of those faithful and unfaithful fathers. Without a father Josué seems in trouble with language, words, letters, and the ability to correspond with the world around him. In this he seems an almost wild child, like those in Francois Truffaut's *Wild Child* (1970), Werner Herzog's *The Enigma of Kaspar Hauser* (1974), and Yorgos Lanthimos's *Dogtooth* (2009). Unlike those barely or strangely articulate children, however, Josué lives in an impoverished urban world of angry or empty language. Only at the end of the film, united with formerly unknown brothers, does he begin to discover the power and mobility of language when he discovers magical correspondences through this new family of brothers, introduced to him through the nonsensical joy of a linguistic tongue twister: "*Lá de trás de minha casa, Tem um pé de umbu botando, Umbu verde, umbu maduro, Umbu seco, umbu secando*" ("Behind my house, There's an umbu tree laying, Green umbu, ripe umbu, Umbu dry, umbu drying," but translated freely in English subtitles as the tongue-twisting "Peter Piper picked a peck of pickled peppers.") Even or especially the dexterous pronunciation of words becomes a verbal and social empowerment.

Rarely do we think about the status of speech or writing in a movie as the thematic center of a film; instead, the articulation and presentation of words tends mostly to serve and support the image or soundtrack, shaping characterization or narrative motivations. Yet words in themselves, especially as they are materialized in letters have been at times the center of films, most notably in the many epistolary movies, from *Letter to an Unknown Woman* (1948) to *Sunless* (1983) to *You've Got Mail* (1998). In many of these films, letters frequently make visible emotions, conflicts, and ideas as distinctive material registers of the drama. They become, I think, a version of what Michel Chion calls iconogenic: "written words that engender more of the story, that take a physical narrative form, and ... lead us on the screen to the reality they evoke" (6). In *Central Station*, despite their foregrounding as letters and however easy to take for granted, words become the story itself, the difficult vehicle for the many different correspondences between characters and their sometimes inability to find with those words correspondences with others and other realities.

From the start, longing pervades the entire atmosphere of the film's narrative—longings for lost fathers, for broken families, for dead friends, and for missing children, longings made even more intense and important by the failure of words to express those longings, to find an interlocutor, to find a reader or listener for those letters, to create a correspondence of any kind with another person, another world, another existence. At the conclusion of the film, as Dora departs on a bus, she gathers the ubiquitous atmosphere that swirls around and through words when Dora reflects, "I long for everything."

The force of that longing and the hope it hides begins to peak and speak, however, toward the conclusion of the film, when the two travelers arrive at the Pilgrimage of Virgin Mary at Candlelight where worshippers flock to the site to seek the light of wisdom in the midst of dark despair, where both spiritual and real mothers search for and pray for absent fathers. In the midst of this spiritual gathering, without money or food, desperate and frustrated, the communicative possibilities of words falter and become a curse.

Dora turns angrily on her temporary ward who has brought her to this destitution, verbally attacking Josué, the curse now attached vindictively to his loss of parents who may have provided him with words but now become the denunciatory words of hostility and condemnation: "Your parents should never have had you. . . . You're a curse, you're a curse," she shouts as he dashes away down the road. No father, no parents, the only language Josué inhabits is the non-language of the curse, a child Caliban in Brazil.

Tracked in a medium close-up through a vast nighttime sea of lit candles, as if in a maze of rabid devotion, Dora races after the fleeing Josué, shouting his name through the mass of chanting Christian pilgrims, all clothed in white and beseeching help from the Virgin Mother in a montage of faces and bodies. Longing across multiple levels, from the physical to the economic to the spiritual, corresponding to each other in the darkness. She then enters a building packed with mumbling individuals, entreating different icons, photos, statues, that fill the walls and tables as silent conversants with desperate pilgrims. Collages of loved ones and icons of Christ hang from the ceiling and fill the walls and tables, as medium close-ups move through humming pleas for comfort and hope. An extreme low-angle close-up of a man who chants fervently, "Fill the darkness with light, Lord." Dora wanders through the flickering yellow light as if in a daze, as if in a dark labyrinth, those measured registers of Swedenborgian spirituality now a twisted hubbub. Fireworks of lights swirl and explode outside above the cheering pilgrims, while inside Dora's point of view spins rapidly through flash pans illuminated by the sea of candles—before she collapses on the floor, lost to Josué and lost to herself.

Loss, though, is a passageway to human compassion and solidarity. After Josué soon finds Dora's collapsed body, there is a cut to an empty, dusty street the following morning where he sits by her prone body before small houses, her head on his lap in a pose of affection and care, a secular pietà. In a medium shot, she awakens, clutches and pats his knee with a faint smile, and then turns to look deeply into his eyes. He has become the father-son of a fragile older mother. Another cut finds the two tossing rocks in a can, while a man preaches about the devil and evil. A boy plays the guitar. Two gypsy women ask Dora for money to have her fortune read, but that is not her spirit world. Within these daily rumblings and ramblings through this village, Josué suddenly recognizes the power of a correspondence between the religious and the physical worlds. He stands before a diorama of a replica of a sainted priest where for three dollars a person one can take a photo with the saint and include it in a letter sent to him. For Josué, the economics of this cardboard saint becomes, with passion and humor, a horizontal portal between the saintly and secular, the possibility of a bond and correspondence with the world he has always lacked and with the two mothers he has lost. Swedenborg after capitalism.

Almost immediately, the now entrepreneurial Josué convinces a young woman in need that Dora will write a letter to the saint for her and send it for only one dollar. Thus, Dora's letter-writing begins again, but now as part of a dramatically different register: as part of a mutual relationship with Josué, she discovers a new belief and faith in the words she writes and he in his ability to serve her as her agent and partner in the midst of their spiritual, familial, and economic redemption. In a medium close-up, he negotiates between the two women. In a medium long shot, Josué barks in front of Dora's stand as she writes for the young woman, "Letters! Send a Letter Home!" Correspondence returns but now as a link based in mutual trust and commitment. A surprised bearded man asks in close-up, "One buck?," and Josué answers with delighted confidence, "Two if you want us to post it." A cut to Dora biting her lip— in concern or surprise or perhaps pride. Emanuel Swedenborg, reincarnated as a financial broker, corresponds now across the different social, personal, and material realms of the expanding line of a community faith.

There follows a montage of close-ups that parallels and contrasts the opening montage of Dora writing letters in the Central Station.

Josué sits at the table with Dora, collecting the money they desperately need to continue their journey in search of a father. A young bride asks Dora to write a saint to say, "I'm fulfilling the vow I made to come here if Benicio agreed to marry me." A cut to a close-up of the smiling Josué, glowing and winking at Dora. As the camera moves forward for an extreme close-up on her smiling face, another young woman tells her to write "Thank you, Jesus, for answering my prayers. My husband has stopped drinking." A bearded man shakes his head vigorously with delight, dictating, "I am now the happiest man in the world." An older man whose face speaks of experience and duration writes warmly about his missing son. Another vibrant young woman sends love to her mother, Maria Adalgiza Bezzera. Another to her fiancé in Sao Paulo. A man removes his hat to have her write "Thank you, baby Jesus, for answering our prayers. Thank you for bringing us rain this year." A litany of human need and gratitude, written with words that move with emotional trust and faith, not only spoken to saints but also written to each other, also written to Dora and Josué.

Josué and Dora celebrate their money by having a photo taken of themselves together in front of the diorama with the priest-saint, a frontal shot with the cardboard figure of the saint between them, an almost comical metaphor for the horizontal passageways that they have crossed and that has now bonded them. These letters will be sent, not tossed in the trash or crumpled in a desk drawer. For those dictating the words and for the writer of those words, they will correspond to something unseen but known, something made material. Like a missing father or like a missing family.

14

Describing . . . Anticipation:
In the Mood for Love
(Wong Kar-wai, 2000)

Most movies build their marketing and distribution campaigns around anticipation, commonly with teasers and stars. Most movies likewise structure their narratives around different kinds of anticipation, commonly with conflict and suspense. In both cases the films themselves respond, in one way or another, to those anticipations with some kind of closure at the end of a film: questions answered, mysteries solved, lovers united. When anticipations are resolved, descriptions discover a retroactive clarity. How, though, does description engage a film that moves relentlessly through repeated and unresolved anticipations, where anticipation becomes a shimmering and evanescent mood, a holding of the breath, a rhythmic blur, a

Describing Cinema. Timothy Corrigan, Oxford University Press. © Oxford University Press 2024.
DOI: 10.1093/oso/9780197625354.003.0015

souvenir of something that never has happened or will happen. How does one describe a mood that never becomes an action, like a rehearsal of a scene that will never be acted on a real stage, which is for me the mesmerizing luxury of Wong Kar-wai's *In the Mood for Love*. The film moves across a series of intermediary back stages, stages of suspension but not of suspense: historical stages from 1962 Hong Kong, through 1963 Singapore, and then 1966 Hong Kong and Angkor, Cambodia; geographical stages through the global city of Hong Kong where international tourist and business types travel continually back and forth between Asia, Europe, Africa, and the Americas; domestic stages, through a cramped boarding house where Mr. Chow and Mrs. Chan meet and where their first encounters occur in tight hallways and on narrow staircases; textual stages, through soundscapes that drift into the past and across various subcultures and eras; and, private stages, through two sets of mismatched married couples, one couple having a sexual affair, a couple mostly invisible except for the rare flash of a back or the sound of a voice, and the other couple the visible center of the film, struggling to resist an increasingly emotional and physical attraction. Layering these different stages, each overlapping the other, this is a sumptuously excruciating film that wants me to describe something that happens on these stages but never takes place.

A doubled secret drifts underneath the boards of these stage floors, both known and resisted: on one level, there is the uncanny realization that the invisible spouses, somewhere else in the world, are involved in that sexual liaison; on another, there is Mr. Chow and Mrs. Chan's refusal to accept or to act upon their own growing passion for each other, which can only be acknowledged through a series of deferred and deflected innuendos, suggestions, slight encounters, and repeated rehearsals. Why this inability to act? Moral codes or public opinion maybe, both signaled in the proper names that they never seem to abandon, creating a distance within their intimacy that can only appear as the strain of anticipation for what will never happen?

Here that excruciating anticipation lives and thrives only where rehearsals can never become performance, where rehearsals and repetitions become intense preparations for a consummation that can never happen, where passion must live only in trenchant but mercurial moods? *In the Mood for Love* describes the endless, perhaps hopeless, effort of approaching those doubled secrets as an always unfulfilled delay. In this cinematic theater of confined and pressing spaces and superimposed zones, the two remarkable and well-known actors (Maggie Chueng and Tony Leung) rehearse again and again within a temporality of expectation where they can only remember or project what might have happened if there had been the possibility of these actors acting, which becomes the presiding atmosphere of a mood, a temporary feeling extended for years or for the length of the film. No wonder I am fixated, like the characters themselves, by the appearances of these two perfectly composed faces and their carefully posed bodies, as if they are always struggling, ineffectually, to act through their skill as actors. Where would Leo Braudy place these actors who seem to straddle a theatrical and cinematic mode of presentation, paralyzed between the theatrical and the naturalistic? Of course, Mrs. Chan flees by herself to the movies regularly, that distilled atmosphere of "what if."

What may be most striking about this film is that it is a melodrama without drama and primarily about the *melos* of mood. Like most melodramas, a coincidence—the spouses of Mr. Chow and Mrs. Chan having an affair with each other—seems so impossibly weird in this global intersection that the tale takes on an atmosphere of unreality, like a dream. Loosely adapted from a 1948 Chinese *wenyi pian* melodrama, *Springtime in a Small Town*, the characters struggle to create themselves within the rituals of a Chinese melodrama, like all those other rituals they play out in the film—as games, dinners, and conversations—yet, in these contemporary times, they are incapable of either articulating or activating the desire that might drive their melodrama to any kind of conclusion, even a tragic one. Rituals without actions or conclusions. All that remains for the two almost lovers is their restraint, suspended within the excessive potential of unacknowledged desire. Ironically, while classic melodramas commonly focus their crises on the extreme difficulty of the characters to express or act on their desire and emotions, here Mr. Chow and Mrs. Chan seem constantly to talk in order to avoid acting on those desires and emotions, placed within static compositions, high-key lighting and highlighting, frames within frames and restrictive blocking. More exactly, in this melodrama, the drama seems to dissipate and deflect into the sumptuous non-diegetic melodies and songs from another time and place, which, like Nat King Cole's version of "Quizás, Quizás, Quizás" ("Perhaps, Perhaps, Perhaps"), signal a repeated state of past and future anticipation that never enters the present time and place and that sings my linguistic tentativeness of describing a state of "living a life of shadows only." Throughout, a brief, minimalist, and repeated string arrangement, called "Yumeji's Theme," a gentle but anxious violin melody, describes with music this state of half-consciousness within rhythmically wandering bodies.

That double-sided secret must be continually displaced into a rehearsed anticipation of themselves that moves front stage, almost nonchalantly, midway through the film. The sequence begins when Mrs. Chan visits the ill Mr. Chow (in room 2046 of his hotel room, a peculiar reference to Wong Kar-wai's 2004 sequel to *In the Mood for Love*, creating a kind of reflexive proleptic gap in the production of a later film whose anticipation mirrors the rehearsal zones of the present film, there but not yet there). Her arrival, described by a rapid montage of low-angle shots of her racing legs and feet across the floor of a shimmering modernist hallway of rectangular shapes, abruptly halts in an unusual shot of her bending over as if she has lost her composure—or perhaps her motivation or perhaps fear or perhaps emotion. So many incidental details interrupt possible action. In response to his surprise that she has come to see him, linked by a series of crosscuts with heads bent and eyes askance, he says, "I didn't think you would come," and she responds with a line that would define their relationship: "We won't be like them," referring to their unfaithful spouses but maybe also to their other selves. And why not?, I wonder. And if not, what *will* they be like? Her receding figure departs down the hallway with her heels clicking out the languorous musical motif of the film and then slowly stopping in a brief freeze frame. Every sound in this film seems almost to overtake the images. Every oneiric movement—along streets, in hallways—seems as if caught in a space where the next step is hesitatingly uncertain. A stylistic of incompleteness.

There are then several frames of medium shots of the two non-lovers, he now recovered from his illness in his room. They co-write contentedly together a story for another genre, a martial arts novel that would offer them the chance to displace the paralysis of their melodramatic crisis into the writing of an active genre, one of Linda Williams's body genre, but oppositional, physical, and, most importantly, active on paper only or at least. The martial and the marital in disturbing dialogue? As the track continues to roam the room, back and forth, it catches glimpses of the smiling Mrs. Chan and then the multiple medium close-up reflections of Mr. Chow, intensely reading and writing their story of physical movements and dexterous passions. A phonograph record plays, and they silently clap to the music, their reflections within the several frames of a dressing-table mirror, multiple images of Mrs. Chan reading from a page, a script for someone else.

Against the strained violins of the theme music, the couple silently mouths a conversation behind the slightly blurred edges of a series of images with textured surfaces of smoke, foregrounded objects, covering curtains, and the traces of patterned wallpaper, as they happily smile, chat, read, and eat, in this other genre, on this other stage, the dream of a romantic couple within an impossibly suspended space where their own images double and overlap with their own selves. Indeed, those textured surfaces and the haunting music that permeates the scene, like the flamboyant and flowered dresses that Mrs. Chan wears throughout the film, describe a world that bristles and glows across its surface, a world they cannot fully enter from the wings into the active space of the martial arts genre that here can only distract them with other more actively dangerous possibilities.

Within this elsewhere theater and its textured fourth wall, Mrs. Chan breaks the silence covered by the soundtrack, addressing the foregrounded back of Mr. Chow—or is it her absent husband? "Tell me honestly," she says as she turns from her bowl of food toward the back of the man next to her. "Do you have a mistress?" The male off-screen voice responds, "You're crazy. Who told you that?" She answers, "Never mind who. Do you or don't you?" as she leans forward into the back of the man who is temporarily her husband. "No." "Don't Lie. Look at Me. . . . I'm asking you if you have a mistress." "Yes," the actor admits. When, I wonder, did this other couple take over the stage?

She stares at him and then pretends to slap him across the face, as the image cuts to a reverse shot of Mr. Chow, who then tries to coach and improve her performance, which may have become too actual, too real, or not real enough: "That's no reaction. If he admits it outright, let him have it," he urges. She sighs, "I wasn't expecting that he'd admit it easily." She turns away and looks down at her food and then off-screen. "Are you alright?" he asks. "I didn't expect it to hurt so much," she admits as she begins to cry and leans over on his shoulder. "This is just a rehearsal," he reminds her as he tries to comfort her. The camera tracks back across the room in shallow focus of blurred reds and flowered patterns, blurs that describe not a space but a psychological and social texture of intense suspension and anticipation, where a rehearsal is so much more than a rehearsal, where rehearsals of the real are painfully difficult. An agonizing mood.

Later, at the conclusion, in Angkor, Cambodia, the fade of time, of the past, of love lost, and of desire deferred, arrives not in one of those overlapping spaces but at a temple and place that is the "empty ruins of someone else's eternity." Here, years later, Mr. Chow "remembers those vanished years. As though looking through a dusty window pane, the past is something he could see, but not touch. And everything he sees is blurred and indistinct." Those remembered rehearsals of the couple settle as the memory of a never realized anticipation where their suppressed passion and identities drift into the missing identities of their respective spouses, whose barely acknowledged betrayal also describes the disabled longing of Mr. Chow and Mrs. Chan, a longing slowed to the rhythmically laborious steps of a difficult rehearsal unsure of a next move. All those delays that shape and propel description now are the essential heart of the film in which, unlike most films, it stops short of the struggle to act and to articulate, resigned in that place of anticipation where anticipation has now become a nostalgia for longing.

Not surprisingly, I remember a passage from the 1984 book *On Longing* by Susan Stewart, my old friend and former colleague, writing about longings, desires, and souvenirs: "The realization of re-union imagined by the nostalgic is a narrative utopia that works only by virtue of its partiality, its lack of fixity and closure: nostalgia is the desire for desire.... The nostalgic dreams of a moment before knowledge and self-consciousness that itself lives on only in the self-consciousness of the nostalgic narrative. Nostalgia is the repetition that mourns the inauthenticity of all repetition and denies the repetition's capacity to form identity" (23-24). Is not the repeatedly rehearsed and inescapable secret of a never found and yet lost love a kind of nostalgic souvenir?

15

Describing . . . Gaming: *The Bourne Ultimatum* (Paul Greengrass, 2007)

The increased rapidity of nonlinear film editing, especially after the so-called digital turn of the 1990s, has become commonplace in the history of contemporary film. In the 2000s, many films had an average shot length close to three or four seconds, while many films made before 1960 could average ten to fourteen seconds between cuts. There are of course other films and tendencies during these periods (including the beautifully contemplative slow cinema movements that hover through the long takes of Terrence Malick or Kelly Reichardt), but there is no denying the stylistic prominence of these rapidly paced films today and the challenges for a viewer to keep pace with the narrative action, let alone to reflect on particular images. To describe these films requires constant verbal, almost physical, attention.

This cinema of quickly shifting actions and unanticipated points of view often resemble the structures and styles of video games (whether or not these films directly reference their resemblances

Describing Cinema. Timothy Corrigan, Oxford University Press. © Oxford University Press 2024.
DOI: 10.1093/oso/9780197625354.003.0016

to these interactive games or sometimes as their actual adaptation or remake of those games). Which made me recall John Belton's remark about *The Bourne Ultimatum*, "Game logic rules, and Jason Bourne is an expert at playing games" (413). Describing a film like *The Bourne Ultimatum* (or any of the films in that series) might consequently suggest that, as Alex Galloway argued about video games, "what used to be the act of reading is now the act of doing" (3). In this, Galloway makes the useful distinction between "expressive acts" and "move acts" in video games. Yet in the game of describing these rapidly edited films, those two acts merge in the rhetoric of a descriptive language that must make each quick move an expressive verbal action.

For me, there seems consequently to be something appropriate, perhaps necessary, in watching the *Bourne* films on my laptop, where there is a certain physical flexibility and mobility with which this screen mirrors and engages the constant speed, shifting overlapping, and rapid interactivity of these films. Across these *Bourne* films about an amnesiac and traumatized secret agent pursued by the CIA, his forgotten CIA agency, and in search his lost identity, description needs to create expressive move acts, as a quick and sometimes fragmented syntax reflecting the visual composition of the films. Like Bourne's flight to survive, with descriptive execution, to move is itself expression; describing the game is itself the meaning of the film. In this execution, I am a second-person shooter—as writer.

A particularly dynamic example of my position, the Waterloo Station sequence in *The Bourne Ultimatum* (2007) weaves the two acts as a kind of critical ultimatum and quintessential gaming challenge. Beginning approximately fifteen minutes into the film, when the CIA identify and surveille a British reporter, Simon Ross, the sequence lasts a quick thirteen or so minutes through a series of cuts and flash pans, amounting to over 400 shifts and misdirections, edits averaging approximately 1.8 seconds each. There are five key players: Bourne; the eponymous protagonist; Ross, the sympathetic

British reporter; the Director of the CIA, who pursues Bourne through numerous electronic extensions or mobile "Operatives"; and a fifth player, the "Asset," an assassin who, in this game, is Bourne's equal as a player.

The Director is my opponent; Bourne is my surrogate. The Operatives and the Asset are less characters than figures in play, to be avoided, manipulated, or overcome. Indeed, Bourne too is barely more than a phantom figure (at least in the first few of the *Bourne* films), without a memory or identity but with the extraordinary skills of a player who seems to act and react more with visceral instincts than with reflective intelligence. In a sense they are all "applications," and I am Bourne's affective extension, with perhaps more perspective than the other players but armed only with the eyes and ears of the screen and, most importantly, with a descriptive language to articulate my engagement. If for Galloway there are, unified and overlapping, "two basic types of action in video games: machine actions and operator actions" (5), here the screen of the film is the machine that language must try to operate.

The control center gathers these different players in and around the multiple screens within the U.S. Langley CIA center. Watching the frenzy of screen images within an arena of agents before a bank of screens in the foreground and background, the Director responds to the representational—imagistic and audial—splits and divides that energize and complicate the game. Underpinning the action is the recurrent tension between sight and sound: with mounting urgency the Director barks, "Where's my picture," and then moments later, "Why am I not hearing this?" as the image cuts to Ross picking up a *Guardian* office phone and answering the call from the new audio player, Bourne, who tells Ross that he has been "reading your stories." While interior windows speed across the backdrop of the train he has boarded, Bourne delivers his moves sharply: "Waterloo Station south entrance, thirty minutes, come alone." More frames intersect: the window frame in Ross's cab overlays the computer frames of the CIA office: as the velocity of the different moves increases, the audio language picks up the pace to follow and link the shifts: "Where's he going? . . . Ok guys let's work it. . . . He's on the move." An aerial long shot above Waterloo Station appears like a maze or puzzle, a visual analogue for the screen and game space. Their screens, like mine, feature amplified computer clicks that move the images through an on-screen graphic command to show the exterior and interior of Waterloo Station, an immediately intensified gaming space where people and trains are in constant motion. Another rapid zoom to the determined movement of Bourne as he enters the station, supported by the driving rhythms of a soundtrack that coordinates and centralizes his movements. With difficulty I visually keep up. A cut to the CIA station with a four-quadrant screen next to a duplicated enlarged screen of Ross on the move. Which screen to follow? My vision jumps, divided. Back in the street with Ross, who appears through crosscuts with alternative angles and images provided by the Operatives as "eyeballs on the street." Even this dimension, however, quickly shifts in this film across the command "mobile one I need audial" directed at another motorcycled Operative whose "audio is engaged," so that an image appears on a desk screen of a taxi arriving. "Mobile one should have it," a voice confirms.

Is this a version of Paul Virilio's non-place where the visual limits the actions of the main players and so requires another dimension, audio depth and perspective? Is Bourne an interface that becomes metaphoric of a Virilio's "integral cinematism" that locates speed within a series of fast, constant, and valueless transitions as the disintegration of space. Here "the perspectival effects of classical ornaments and the cinematic characteristics of certain styles . . . is replaced by integral cinematism, an absolute transitivity, involving the complete and thorough decomposition of reality and property" (Lost Dimension 118). Here speed induces an ephemerality that in turn produces disappearance and blindness across many levels from the psychological to the industrial—and possibly the ideological.

Inside the densely crowded station and the densely crowded CIA game room, the active and passive players move to the next level, with the Director making a decisive move: "Give me eyes at Waterloo Station, put everyone in play, activate the Asset." A cut to the lounging Asset, somewhere, receiving a close-up mobile command to proceed to enter the station space; he equips himself and begins his moves down a hotel hallway. An aerial of the moving taxi, a close-up of Ross, and a cut to CIA headquarters. A computer-screen map of the game streets (like a Google map) animates with bright colors the otherwise shadowy action. Bourne arrives at the Waterloo game space, followed by a rapid zoom on the movements of different Waterloo surveillance cameras, active and predatory instruments of a machine that generates images. Visually he/we are in danger of being outnumbered by the image machine.

Bourne counters with the purchase of a prepaid cell phone to activate his participation, an audio tool to counter the dominant visuals. He connects with a close-up of Ross whose desperate plea, "What the hell is going on?," is that of an inexperienced, confused, and inevitably vulnerable player, doomed by his lack of skill. Bourne again delivers quick information and instructions to Ross outside, pursued by the Operatives: "Across the street a van. . . . There's a man in a second story room . . . watching you. . . . There's a bus stop . . . 50 meters to your left walk towards it . . . turn around." Cut to the Director's Langley team where the anxious voices and editing attempt to adjust to Bourne's audio: "It's not his phone. . . . Where the hell did he get another phone?" "Team B" moves to intercept Ross.

The battle of competing screens and technologies mounts: an overlay of the CIA screens, a medium shot of Bourne on a phone, and secondary video images of Ross at a bus stop. The commands accelerate to keep pace with the images, as Bourne's directional moves intentionally misleads the Operatives to a decoy player at the bus stop: "Do not let him get out of sight," the Director commands, but Bourne is well out of sight as an audial player. Bourne moves his decoy: "Who's the guy in the blue hood? Is that his contact?"

the Director shouts. Bourne counters, directing his own co-player through more evasions: "A bus will be there in 10 seconds, when it stops I want you to walk . . . to an overpass. There's a newsstand. Stop there . . . to get further instructions. Get ready to move." Rapid cuts as the Operatives arrive from various directions, pursuing that false decoy in the blue hood "on the move," whom they quickly intercept, drug, and drag off the bus. Flash to Bourne who eliminates another Operative on an interior staircase. Bourne wins Level One, which even the CIA acknowledges: "What was that? . . . We lost all communication . . ."

Inside Waterloo Station, the velocity of the contest continues to intensify, amidst anonymous crowds who become physical and visual obstacles and covers at this center of rapid transit. With the alert "target's on the move," the Director signals this next level. To keep up, my language must approximate theirs and become urgent, propelled by the nonstop questions ("Last known position, please?") as we are swept up into the space of "a surveillance nightmare." The Director extends his power as he appropriates "all of CTV's eyes" in the station. A female agent at a CIA game station rapidly types new commands; a speeding car arrives with the Asset and his extended-techno-first-person point of view. Bourne confronts Ross at the station entrance in a quick shot/counter-shot exchange: "Who's your source?" "Why are these people after me?" A flash zoom to the other Operatives entering the station; Bourne responds, "We have to move." Rapid cuts follow, through surveillance cameras and the multiple duplicating screens of the CIA command post. The Director shouts: "Where the hell is he people?" The player-phantom Bourne, a disappearing image.

The logic of the game machine edits and shifts, without motivation it seems, between unmoored points of view, eyelines, flash pans, and players or nonplayers alike. Human beings become obstacles within the unsettling anxiety of who sees, who doesn't, who plays, and which is which team. Bourne retakes control of the game and commands Ross: "Tie your shoe . . . in 4, 3, 2, 1, standup," while the Director senses his disadvantage: "We can't afford to lose this guy, people!" Countering the Director's commands, Bourne continues to master the space and the actions: "That line you're on is good. Stay on line." The Director reacts: "Get me a feed in there.... Tell me what's going on," while Ross panics and breaks free of Bourne's control and commands. A fatal, rogue mistake in this game, as he is chased through a kiosk by the Operatives.

Through a series of rapid cuts in a back staircase, Bourne intercepts and takes down the four Operatives through the execution of a series of quick visual and physical moves. Close-ups bring the Asset into the space, armed with a scope and rifle for his entry into the game as the primary opponent, as the Director's audio works to control the space: "Block all the exits, give the Asset a green light." A cut between the Asset and several subjective, first-person shots of Bourne searching the crowds for Ross. As the Director moves to "kill the [surveillance] cameras," the Asset positions his rifle behind another screen of a billboard with opening and closing slats with different advertisements, while he looks to the cell phone screen to retrieve and identify his targets, Bourne and Ross. All these characters appear primarily as images on someone's screen; to be captured as an image is to lose, to be deleted.

The Asset searches the moving crowds where Ross suddenly breaks from the control of Bourne: "I'm going for it." Another wrong move. Acting independently as his own player now, outside the trained skills of Bourne, he is shot multiple times by the Asset and left anonymously for dead among the crowd of frantic bystanders. As Bourne flees he too now becomes a point-of-view image through the rifle-scope circular of the Asset, who pursues him helter-skelter within an empty image, looking for his target in the crowd. In this game, to designate and identify a competing player within a challenger's techno point of view is to win through the dominating force of that perspective, its skills, and the images it produces. Disappearing into the faceless blur of the station crowds, Bourne survives, I'd argue, precisely because of his anonymous identity, an identity without an image, a phantom identity in a vision machine through which Bourne is able to evade the moving screens and images of all his competitors. An unlocatable player. The Asset quickly packs his weapon in close-up and flees the scene for another platform to be opened later in the film, while Bourne pursues him in a chase sequence down staircases, onto streets, and into a tube station, before the Asset disappears onto a moving train, whisking him away through the window frames of the train that disappear like rapidly edited film frames. No one ultimately wins here but the cinematic gaming machine. I wait with unresolved expectations, the next level, the new players, the next screens.

16

Describing . . . The Tactile: *Adam*
(Maryam Touzani, 2019)

Films invite or resist description in different ways, and those that
resist do so in a variety of ways. Experimental films, films with minimal dialogue, and so-called unwatchable films can all complicate
acts of description in how they delimit, eschew, subvert, or foreground imagistic textuality and narrative language.[1] Then there's
the problem of "missing films," movies that have a very brief distribution period or have disappeared from circulation altogether
(problems that have been somewhat mitigated by the internet and
streaming platforms).

Many so-called festival films often fit the categories of resistant
or missing films. These are those sometimes convoluted or difficult

---

[1] About the latter, see the fascinating collection *Unwatchable*.

Describing Cinema. Timothy Corrigan, Oxford University Press. © Oxford University Press 2024.
DOI: 10.1093/oso/9780197625354.003.0017

narrative films that make their initial and often brief appearances at film festivals from Cannes and Toronto to Berlin and Sundance or at many of the hundreds of other film festivals around the world. As Thomas Elsasser has pointed out, in the last couple of decades especially, these diverse and global festival films have arguably developed as a recognizable genre in their own right with distinctive narrative constructions, auteurist labels, and creative stylistics that distinguish them from more mainstream films and often challenge audiences to view them across different cultural landscapes with fresh eyes. For efforts to describe them, they can also pose another challenge: for many of these films, there can be a considerable lag time between seeing the film at a festival and its reappearance in a theater or on a streaming site, so that the many months (or even years) before a film might be re-seen makes description of that film by the original festival viewers the challenge of articulating a missing or fading object or experience. No doubt this challenge can also be true of more everyday experiences when, for instance, we wish to describe a scene or sequence in a film that other people have not seen, so that festival films, in their delayed or missed appearance, may simply highlight and foreground the larger problem of describing a movie unseen by readers or interlocutors.

For me, Maryam Touzani's 2019 *Adam* not only presented many of these common challenges to description but also had those obstacles compounded by its unexpected delayed theatrical release during the COVID pandemic.[2] Especially for this film and for my own eagerness to tell people about it after I had seen it at the 2019 Cannes International Film Festival and before the film eventually arrived at other film festivals and later on a few streaming sites, the difficulty of describing the film or a sequence from it was compounded exponentially by the physical and emotional intensity of its barely dialogic sequences, where images and sounds

---

[2] Thanks to Strand Releasing for making the film available to me while waiting for its pandemic-delayed U.S. distribution.

overwhelm words, straining descriptions with a sensual tactility that can seem to refuse words in the film and in response to it (so breathlessly continued in Touzani's more recent 2022 *Blue Caftan*). Tightly closed within its unusually constricted mise-en-scène of a Moroccan home, serving as a bakery, and a narrative with minimal dramatic action, the bodies, clothing, gestures, and objects breathe with a physical presence where words barely touch each other across so many dense walls of silence. Touzani describes this physical and emotional depth and intensity: "I wanted my camera to be so close to the characters, that we forget that this camera exists, that we can really penetrate their souls, penetrate their beings . . . really be them for an hour and a half to understand them. Penetrate their intimacy, without being in something voyeuristic, break down all the barriers between us, the audience, and these two women" (quoted in Ponsard). In this film, sight and language defer to touch.

Adam recounts the tale of a young, pregnant Moroccan woman, Samia, who wanders door to door in Casablanca, looking for work and housing while she awaits the birth of her out-of-wedlock child. Rejected at different doorways again and again, she makes eye contact from the street with the eight-year-old Warda whose mother Abla eventually but reluctantly, following the entreaties of her daughter, gives Samia shelter. At first, this is shelter only for a night, but eventually she is allowed to stay longer, working with Alba in her house/bakery, as she waits for the baby's birth.

In this shadowy enclosed home, permeated by an atmosphere of loss and anger, palpitating viscerally and silently through Abla's bitter memory of the untimely death of her husband, the condensed, quiet space seems to exaggerate every gesture, movement, and glance. A slow cinema that is only a slowdown of typical dramatic action, with a quiet pacing counterpointed by a visual and audial surface that shimmers tentatively and tensely, like Warda's fingers touching gently across Samia's pregnant belly, making even the shared kneading of bread by the two women at first too fast and then slowed to the tactile movements of hands kneading a succulent mound of moving dough that swallows the rhythmic hands and fingers, a kneading as poignant and emotional as any excessively dramatic, romantic, or talky romance. Perhaps here is an especially visceral example of what Laura Marks terms "haptic visuality" (xi) or a product of what Jennifer Barker has called the "tactile eye" where touch can supersede or even overwhelm words and meaning, where seeing itself becomes a kind of touching.

In this Casablanca, the corporeal tangibility of looking is triangulated between the three generations of women, Abla, Warda, and Samia, to create neither a balanced nor a competitive shot/counter-shot exchange between mothers, daughters, and rivals but rather a continual circulation of affects that will not easily settle down. In this Casablanca, the dynamic of "here's looking at you" turns that historically nostalgic phrase inside out, so that the alternately anguished and delighted dance of these looks concretizes as a vibrant—and sometimes ferocious—caress that collapses into nothing to say. Perhaps this is also about Ulrich Gumbrecht's notion of a production of a presence which meaning cannot convey, of a world where sensual "presence effects" might overtake "meaning effects" (xv) and where that production contains the etymology of the word "production" as to tangibly "bring forth" (17). In Adam, the word "touching" describes here both a traditional sensibility and a radical semantics precisely across the physical and linguistic notion of "to produce," a phrase that vibrates metaphorically and powerfully through this narrative about a young woman about to give birth to a new Adam.

Midway through the film, something unexpected happens, triggered by a song from Abla's past, wafting the two women together in motion, wordlessly, sensually as it pulls Abla's lost self from within her into a movement of skin, hands, arms, eyes. Within the place of the stiffening silence that separates the two women across the room, in the chiaroscuro shadows of a quiet kitchen that opens onto the contrasting rumblings of a Casablanca street, the occasional patter of the *msemen* bread being prepared on a grill vibrates through the space. In the crosscuts between two medium shots of Abla and Samia, waves of light quietly vibrate in the room, according to Touzani, back through the surfaces of Caravaggio, Vermeer, and Georges de la Tour, bringing layers of a lost life into this place. A radio program of male voices murmurs in the background, almost a white noise, almost speaking to a space outside this space, broadcasting to nowhere in this room. A shot drifts to the left from the darkly clad and shadowed Abla to the brightly yellow-patterned dress of Samia at the grill.

Eyes askance, Samia glances toward Abla and toward the window where an unseen customer arrives and asks Abla, for "a *msemen* with cheese." Casually watching the exchange at the window, Samia turns with decided eyes and a slight frown toward the unseen radio/tape player and then moves determinedly toward it. With a sharp glance back at Abla, Samia changes the news commentary to the high-pitched song of a female singer. There is then a cut to the back of Abla carefully and quickly preparing the *msemen* at the window. Without turning, Abla says flatly, "Put the [news] show back on, please." Looking down at the food she's preparing, also refusing eye contact, Samia responds casually, "You're not listening. This is more cheerful." Refusing, for whatever reasons in the corners of her mind or in her isolated corner of the room, Abla's voice-off curtly answers: "No, put the show back on." With a slightly annoyed glance back, Samia changes the station back to the news show.

Another cut back to Abla who takes the customer's money, then back to Samia who retrieves a cassette tape of Abla's formerly favorite singer, Warda Al-Jazairia, a tape, that she had secretly taken earlier, a tape that had been hidden and buried away since the death of Abla's husband, a tape of a softly rhythmic and poignant song repressed and buried through the pain and trauma of loss. Samia looks off-screen toward Abla; Samia's brilliantly deep dark eyes go up and then down, bristling with thought and confrontation across a medium close-up. She turns determinedly to the cassette player above the grill, inserts the tape, starts the song, and then turns her now penetrating eyes back across the edges of the frame toward Abla, waiting for and insisting on a reaction, a look infused with a song that must be recognized and confronted.

Then a cut to Alba's slight but infuriated reaction, as her head rises in anger, taut with restrained shock, her expression stony but with ferocious vibrations across her smooth skin, barely contained by the close-up. Cheek bones flex and ripple in the glow of soft light as she turns. A confused or perplexed or desperate expression? This will be violent, I think; this will be a Hollywood showdown. Her eyes descend to the floor: "Turn that off," she snaps. A reverse shot of the face of Samia, returning her look, head up, eyes bright with an idea, with a personality that won't be denied love and passion for herself or for others. She knows where she's going, shakes her head with a small gesture that travels like a woken slap across the room. "No, I won't turn it off." Abla, now seething with anger, refuses the eyeline of Samia's direct look, eyes that would surely put in motion more of the turbulence that now rocks her as a response to the call of the song. A more insistent "Turn it off now!" becomes less another command than a desperate plea to stop what is slowly becoming an excruciatingly physical pain, the music tearing, as Samia's eyes penetrate her skin. Samia's offscreen "No" erupts through the kitchen, and Abla, with emotion shaking her face almost imperceptibly, eyes fluttering rapidly as if to refuse to see, as if to beat back what her eyes hear, moves quickly off-screen toward Samia. She rushes to turn off the music, Samia grabs her wrists, as she repeats with barely articulated ferocity, "I said turn it off!" A reverse shot of the Samia who, equally determined, replies: "I won't turn it off." They lock in a struggle, eyes and eyelids moving rapidly toward and away from each other, face to face. There is not looking at you; this is looking penetratingly through each other.

Samia grabs and overpowers Abla's flaying hands, which move desperately like someone possessed, with twisting arms struggling to pull away from Samia's grasp. An over-the-shoulder shot of Samai's stoic face as she holds tightly onto Abla's shoulders; a cut to their faces now inches apart as Abla almost screams, "I said turn it off!" The power of close-ups like these, spans, I know, a history of movies from Béla Balázs's soul-searching faces through Ingmar Bergman's devouring women, but these are not souls exposed nor are they personas absorbing each other, as Samia, now the pregnant midwife of another woman's lost emotions, lost body, demands: "You're going to listen." Music here is skin.

Extreme close-ups of their faces face-off into each other within the waves of music. Abla's eyes and expression begin to fall like skin melting away, her face and rapidly blinking eyes losing their habitual sternness in a slow emotional collapse. The body writhes against itself as an angry resistance to years of heartbreak and sorrow and falls into the flow of music as now and then and forever, between a lover past and a mother to be. The two women begin slowly to sway to the music, the close-up of Samia looking intently down at the face of Abla, now unseeing the woman before her but feeling the partner forever inside her. Abla makes one last effort to shake herself free, as her body and arms convulse and twitch, and their two faces almost touch in an extreme close-up.

The camera has disappeared into some deeper realm, some other room of self, which makes me catch my breath in an immersion that has nothing to do with virtual realities. The bound and bonded hands of the two women almost touch across a close-up of their faces while Samia slowly moves and maintains the rhythmic sway of the bodies, a dance that melds the touch of the two women together. Pans of Abla's confused eyes, clenched fists, and their now swaying shoulders. The pregnant Samia eyes her like a mother teaching her child about her own past and how to feel it, just as the child Warda taught her mother, Abla, to open her door to the wandering young woman looking for shelter. Three generations of women, waiting to be born, bound by their touch, in Casablanca 2019.

Samia places her arms around Abla, continuing to move both their bodies to the music, as the crumbling body of Abla gives it-self to Samia and the music engulfs her, her eyes down to both surrender and welcome a lost self, moving back into the home of her body. Her mouth quivers, her eyes closed, released, she clutches her womb, another womb, gently, and begins to weep and sway within a quiet, reborn emotion. As Samia retreats to the faded background of the image, Abla's face relaxes into a soft glow of emotion drifting to its surface, as if in a trance, her head turning rhythmically and blending into the music. Her eyes open, her mouth opens, her skin opens.

Yes, before and after Samia surreptitiously leaves Abla's house later with her new baby, under the dark shadow of uncertainty, this new *Adam* is no doubt a film also about women's rights, about the repressive abortion laws in Morocco, about conclusions and futures with dangling and difficult choices not known. All of these other important dimensions, however, first bristle on the surface of skins and fingers where to touch or to be touched feelingly is to see oneself.

Works Cited

Adorno, T. W. *Minima Moralia: Reflections from Damaged Life*. Trans. E. F. N. Jephcott London: Verso, 1974.

Adorno, T. W. "The Essay as Form." *Notes to Literature*. Vol. 1. New York: Columbia Univ. Press, 1991, 3–23.

Agee, James. *Agee on Film*. Vol. 1. New York: Grosset and Dunlap, 1967.

Baer, Nicholas, Maggie Hennenfield, Laura Horak, and Gunnar Iversen. *Unwatchable*. New Brunswick: Rutgers Univ. Press, 2019.

Balsom, Erika. *Ten Skies*. Melbourne: Fireflies Press, 2021.

Barker, Jennifer. *The Tactile Eye: Touch and the Cinematic Experience*. Berkeley: Univ. of California Press, 2009.

Barthes, Roland. *S/Z*. Trans. Richard Miller. New York: Hill and Wang, 1974.

Barthes, Roland. *Empire of Signs*. Trans. Richard Howard. New York: Farrar, Straus and Giroux, 1982.

Barthes, Roland. "Leaving the Movie Theater." *Rustle of Language*. New York: Hill and Wang, 1986. Pp. 345–349.

Baudry, Jean Louis. "Le dispositif." *Communications* 23 (1975): 56–72.

Bazin, André. "Theater and Cinema." In his *What Is Cinema?* Vol. 1. Berkeley: Univ. of California Press, 1967. Pp. 76–124.

Bazin, André. "Bicycle Thief." In his *What Is Cinema?* Vol. 2. Berkeley: Univ. of California Press, 1967. Pp. 47–60.

Bellour, Raymond. "The Unattainable Text." *Screen* 16.3 (Autumn 1975): 19–28.

Belton, John. *American Cinema/American Culture*. 4th ed. New York: McGraw-Hill, 2013.

Bersani, Leo, and Ulysses Dutoit. *Forms of Being: Cinema/Aesthetics/Subjectivity*. London: BFI, 2004.

Bordwell, David. *The Rhapsodes: How 1940s Critics Changed American Film Culture*. Chicago: Univ. of Chicago Press, 2016.

Braudy, Leo. *The World in a Frame: What We See in Films*. 2nd ed. Chicago: Univ. of Chicago Press, 1984.

Brinkema, Eugenie. *The Forms of Affect*. Durham: Duke Univ. Press, 2014.

Cavell, Stanley. *The World Viewed: Reflections on the Ontology of Film*. Enlarged Edition. Cambridge: Harvard Univ. Press, 1979.

Chaudhuri, Una. *Staging Place: The Geography of Modern Drama*. Ann Arbor: Univ. of Michigan Press, 1997.

Chion, Michel. *Words on Screen*. Ed. and Trans. Claudia Gorbman. New York: Columbia Univ. Press, 2017.

154 WORKS CITED

Corrigan, Timothy. *A Cinema Without Walls: Movies and Culture After Vietnam.* London: Routledge, 1991.

Daney, Serge. *La rampe: Cahier critique 1970–1982*, Paris: Gallimard, 1996.

De Certeau, Michel. "Walking in the City." In *The Practice of Everyday Life.* Trans. Steven Rendall. Berkeley: Univ. of California Press, 1984.

Deleuze, Gilles. *Cinema 2: The Time-Image.* Trans. Hugh Tomlinson and Robert Galeta. Minneapolis: Univ. of Minnesota Press, 1989.

Deleuze, Gilles. *The Fold: Leibniz and the Baroque.* Trans. Tom Conley. Minneapolis: Univ. of Minnesota Press, 1993.

De Quincey, Thomas. "On the Knocking at the Gate in *Macbeth.*" *The Collected Writings of Thomas De Quincey.* Ed. David Masson. Vol. 10. Edinburgh: Adam and Charles Black, 1890. Pp. 389–394.

Doty. Mark. *The Art of Description: The World into Word.* Minneapolis: Graywolf Press, 2010.

Dyer, Richard. "Entertainment and Utopia." In *Only Entertainment.* London: Routledge, 2002. Pp. 19–35.

Elasaesser, Thomas. *European Cinema: Face to Face with Hollywood.* Amsterdam: Amsterdam Univ. Press, 2005.

Friedberg, Anne. *Window Shopping: Cinema and the Postmodern.* Berkeley: Univ. of California Press, 1994.

Galloway, Alex. *Gaming: Essays on Algorithmic Culture.* Minneapolis: Univ. of Minnesota Press, 2006.

Geertz, Clifford. "Thick Description: Toward an Interpretive Theory of Culture" in *The Interpretation of Cultures.* New York: Basic Books, 1973. Pp. 3–30.

Gumbrecht, Hans Ulrich. *Production of Presence, What Meaning Cannot Convey.* Stanford, CA: Stanford Univ. Press, 2004.

Hainge, Greg. *Noise Matters: Towards an Ontology of Noise.* London: Bloomsbury, 2013.

Heffernan, James A. W. *Museum of Words: The Poetics of Ekphrasis from Homer to Ashbery.* Chicago: Univ. of Chicago Press, 2004.

Heidegger, Martin. *On the Way to Language.* Trans. Peter D Hertz. New York: Harper & Row, 1971.

Kalmus, Natalie M. "Color Consciousness." In *Color, The Film Reader.* Ed. Angela Dalle Vacche and Brian Price. New York: Routledge, 2006. Pp. 24–29.

Kaufman, Gerald. *Meet Me in St. Louis.* London: BFI, 1994.

Kauffmann, Stanley. *Regarding Film: Criticism and Comment.* Baltimore: Johns Hopkins Univ. Press, 2001.

Léger, Nathalie. *Suite for Barbara Loden.* London: Les Fugitive, 2015.

Lukács, Georg. *Writer and Critic and Other Essays.* Trans. Arthur Kahn. London: Merlin Press, 1970.

Marcus, Sharon, Heather Love, and Stephen Best. "Building a Better Description." *Representations* 135.1 (Summer 2016): 1–21.

Marker, Chris. *Coréenes*. Paris: Editions du Seuil, 1959.

Marks, Laura. *The Skin of the Film: Intercultural Cinema, Embodiment and the Cinema*. Durham: Duke Univ. Press, 2000.

Mavor, Carol. *Black and Blue: The Bruising Passion of Camera Lucida, La Jetée, Sans Soleil, and Hiroshima mon amour*. Durham: Duke Univ. Press, 2012.

Mitchell, W. J. T. "Ekphrasis and the Other." In *Picture Theory: Essays on Visual and Verbal Representation*. Chicago: Univ. of Chicago Press, 1994. Pp. 151–181.

Mulvey, Laura. *Death 24x a Second: Stillness and the Moving Image*. London: Reaktion, 2006.

Nancy, Jean-Luc, and Federico Ferrari, *Being Nude: The Skin of Images*. New York: Fordham Univ. Press, 2014.

Perez, Gilberto. *The Material Ghost: Film and Their Medium*. Baltimore: Johns Hopkins Univ. Press, 1998.

Perkins, V. F. "Must We Say What They Mean?: Film Criticism and Interpretation." *Movie* 34 (1990): 1–6.

Ponsard, Frédéric. "Maryam Touzani's 'Adam' Looks at the Lives of Two Isolated Moroccan Women in a Patriarchal Society." *Euronews* (2/5/2020): https://www.euronews.com/2020/02/05/maryam-touzani-s-adam-looks-at-the-lives-of-two-isolated-moroccan-women-in-a-patriarchal-s.

Prince, Stephen. "Shakespeare Transposed." *Throne of Blood* DVD. New York: Criterion Collection, 2003.

Rothman, William. *Hitchcock: The Murderous Gaze*. Cambridge: Harvard Univ. Press, 1984.

Seigworth, Gregory J., and Melissa Gregg. *The Affect Theory Reader*. Durham: Duke Univ. Press, 2010.

Stern, Lesely. "Writing/Images." *The Cine-Files: A Scholarly Journal of Cinema Studies* 4 (Spring 2013). http://www.thecine-files.com/wp-content/uploads/2013/06/LesleyStern.pdf.

Stevens, Wallace. "The Creation of Sounds." In *Collected Poetry and Prose*. Ed. Frank Kermode and Joan Richardson. New York: Library of America, 1997. Pp. 274–275.

Stewart, Susan. *On Longing: Narratives of the Miniature, the Gigantic, the Souvenir, the Collection*. Durham: Duke Univ. Press, 1992.

Virilio, Paul. *The Vision Machine*. Bloomington: Indiana Univ. Press, 1994.

Virilio, Paul. *The Lost Dimension*. Trans. by Daniel Moshenberg. Los Angeles: Semiotext(e), 2012.

Wagstaff, Christopher. *The Conformist*. London: BFI, 2012.

Williams, Linda. "Film Bodies: Gender, Genre, and Excess." *Film Quarterly* 44. 4 (Summer, 1991): 2–13.

Woolrich, Cornell. *Rear Window*. New York: iBooks, 2001.

Index

For the benefit of digital users, indexed terms that span two pages (e.g., 52–53) may, on occasion, appear on only one of those pages

Smith, Mr. (character in *Meet Me in St. Louis*), 32, 33–36
Smith, Tootie (character in *Meet Me in St. Louis*), 31–34, 35–36
snow people (in *Meet Me in St. Louis*), 31, 32–33
social order, disruption of, 43–44
sounds
 in *Macbeth*, 51
 in *Marriage of Maria Braun, The*, 91–92
 in *Throne of Blood*, 49–50, 51
space(s)
 interior versus exterior, 116–22
 in *Marriage of Maria Braun, The*, 87–88, 89–90
 public versus private, 101–4, 105
 in *Throne of Blood*, 50–51
 See also interiors; place(s)
speechlessness, problem of, 6
spider web of description, 1–25
 affective description, 16–21
 describing cinema, 9–16
 ekphrasis and description, 7–9
 energy of verbal description, models for, 25
 introduction to, 1–3
 pedagogy of description, 4–6
 vertiginous description, 22–25
spirituality
 Pilgrimage of Virgin Mary at Candlelight, 126–27
 spiritual correspondences, 124
Springtime in a Small Town (Chinese *wenyi pian* melodrama), 132–33
stages, types of, 131
stained-glass windows, 79, 80–81, 82–83, 84–85
staircases, symbolism of, 87
Stern, Lesley, 10
Stewart, Alisdair (character in *The Piano*), 109, 112–14
Stewart, Jimmy, 22–23

Stewart, Michael, 100–1, 104
Stewart, Susan, 136
"St. James Infirmary" (jazz trumpet piece), 121–22
St. Louis, in *Meet Me in St. Louis*, 30–31
suicide, 116–22
Suite for Barbara Loden (Léger), 13–14
sumi-e compositions, 46
Sunless (Mussorgsky), 95–96
Sunless (*Sans Soleil*, Marker), 22–23, 93–99, 125–26
surfaces, 82–83
Sutherland, Donald, 79
Swedenborg, Emanuel, 124, 128

the tactile, description of, 145–52
Taste of Cherry (Kiarostami), 116–22
Technicolor process, 77–78
Ten (Kiarostami), 116–17
Ten Skies (Balsom), 12–13
texts
 properly written, 1–2
 real-time experience of, 11
theater
 cinema versus, 1
 drama of theatrics versus reality, 39–40
Throne of Blood (Kurosawa), 45–51
Tiber River, 37–38
time, layering of, 91–92
tongue twisters, 124–25
touching
 as sight, 152
 the tactile, description of, 145–52
 as term, 148
Touzani, Maryam
 Adam, 145–52
 Blue Caftan, 146–47
transactional exchanges, 46–47
transitions, 81